THE CONNECTED MANAGER: LEADERSHIP 101

John P. Nesgoda III

Contents

SECTION 4
UNDERSTAND YOUR ROLE   **134**

Acknowledgments

I want to acknowledge all of my Team Members, Supervisors, Managers, and Directors that I have worked with over the years. You have provided insight, inspiration, and direction, you have been my colleagues, peers, friends, and teachers throughout my career.

To my family for your understanding and support you have provided me over the years. For having to deal with all the late night conference calls, the travelling on business, missed dinners and family events. You have always stood by my side.

I would also like to acknowledge all of the managers and leaders who are reading this book. You are the ones that are making a positive difference every day for your teams, their families, and your organization.

Introduction

Being a connected manager and leader to your team and your organization is crucial for you to succeed. Some of the worst managers were just as insightful as some of the best ones I have had. If you had worked in any business or corporate environment, you will most likely at one point or another encounter the good, the bad, and the ugly.

A little bit about myself, I have been in a leadership position in one form or fashion since 2004. I have worked in all types of environments from small companies to large international organizations. I have worked in some of the most diverse cities in the world. It does not matter what setting in which you work. This material will show how to be a successful leader regardless of the experience you have in a management role.

Being a manager can be one of the most challenging and rewarding roles in any environment. A manager is crucial to any work environment and can take an excellent work environment and turn it into a toxic one or take a lousy work environment into a positive, enjoyable one.

You have taken the first step in becoming a successful modern manager and leader. The material that you will cover includes areas you should focus on and things you should avoid. This material will help you create an environment for your team that is engaged, productive and happy.

"Leadership and learning are indispensable to each other."

- *John F. Kennedy*

SECTION 1

DEFINING A LEADER

Leadership (noun) lead·er·ship - The action of leading a group of people or an organization. "different styles of leadership"

Synonyms: guidance, direction, control, management, superintendence, supervision; guidance, direction, control, management, superintendence, supervision, directorship, governorship, governance, administration, captaincy, control, ascendancy, supremacy, rule, command, power, dominion, influence

1
Leadership Qualities

"If your actions inspire others to dream more, learn more, do more and become more, you are a leader."

- ***John Quincy Adams***

IF YOU HAD TO DEFINE A GOOD MANAGER what are some areas would they excel in? Ultimately, a great leader creates and nurtures their employees. A great leader possesses a clear vision, is courageous, and has integrity, is honest, and shows humility and has a clear focus. He or she is a strategic planner and believes in teamwork.

Leaders do not exist to order employees around. It is essential for a leader to trust your employees to perform their tasks professionally and independently. Spending time with each employee so you get to know the individual and how they fit on your team will help build that trust.

Managers who show great leadership qualities can accomplish amazing things with their teams. Certain leadership qualities not only drive companies but also continuously inspire teams.

Big Five Personality Traits

While there are a number of different models to categorize the characteristics of a leader, the "Big Five" model is the most widely excepted. The traits are openness, conscientiousness, extraversion agreeableness and neuroticism.

There are a number of tests you can take online to see how you score in each of the categories. Keep in mind that personality tests can sometimes help you better understand yourself in order to better ones self. They cannot completely define who you are as person or describe you fully even if they get some things right.

Openness

Openness is a strong predictor of who will become and succeed as a leader. It means you are original, imaginative, daring, you have broad interests and you generally prefer variety over fixed routines.

Conscientiousness

Conscientiousness is the best predictor of both personal and professional success. It's also the strongest predictor of leadership in different contexts, including business, government, and school. It means you are hardworking ambitious, energetic and you like planning things in advance. Conscientiousness, more so than the other Big Five personality traits, is related to leader emergence and effectiveness.

Extraversion

Extroversion is another strong predictor of who will become a leader — though psychologists are increasingly discovering that introverts can do just as well in leadership roles. It means you are sociable, fun-loving, affectionate, friendly, and talkative, you pull your energy from social activities. Out of all the personality traits, extraversion has the strongest relationship with both leader emergence and leader effectiveness. This is not to say that all effective leaders are extraverts, but you are more likely to find extraverts in leadership positions.

Agreeableness

Agreeable people tend to be happier, possibly because they try to avoid negative experiences. On the other hand, *disagreeable* people may be more likely to succeed at work because they're better at getting their ideas heard. It means you are tolerant, sensitive, trusting, kind and warm.

Neuroticism

Neuroticism is also sometimes called Emotional Stability. This dimension relates to one's emotional stability and degree of negative emotions. Neurotic people tend to react to perceived threats and stressful situations. It means you worry a lot, you're moody, irritable temperamental and sometimes anxious.

Accountability

Being a good leader also means being accountable, not only for yourself but for your team as well. Take the good with the bad; we all have setbacks, use them as learning experiences to grow. Accountable leaders do not blame others when things go wrong and take responsibility and take action to improve the situation.

Delegation and Empowerment

It is essential to learn how to delegate. Not all tasks need to be handled by you, most new employees in a leadership role struggle with this. Learning to delegate is one of the hardest things to do, especially when you know you can do it effectively.

It is also crucial to learn how to delegate because when you do, you empower the employee to make their own decisions to complete the task. Stand behind their choices and encourage them and coach when needed.

Honesty

Strong leaders treat people the way they want to be treated. They are extremely ethical and believe that honesty, effort, and reliability form the foundation of success. They embody these values so overtly that no employee doubts their integrity for a minute. They share information openly.

It is important to share information openly. However some topics it is difficult to be transparent. If there is the elephant in the room that they would like to talk about, but can't, tell them you can't but will when the time is right. Honesty creates trust, and there are far few things more import than building trust between yourself and your team.

Empathetic

Empathy is defined as the ability to understand one's perspective and feelings, and experiences. You will not be able to build a team or nurture a new generation of leaders with it as you will not be able to inspire others or create loyalty.

It is important to listen, and truly listen to your people. There are usually hidden emotions behind what the employee is saying. You must be present, put the phone down and give the employee your full attention.

Don't interrupt the employee, and give them time to get their message out. Don't rush to give advice or change the subject. Take a personal interest in people, ask the about what is going on in their lives. Talk to them about their hobbies, families, etc.

Discipline / Self-control

Maintaining self-control and emotional balance is a critical area that all needs must focus on as it maximizes performance especially when dealing with adversity. As a leader, you are more likely to inspire your team instead of being abusive or having to micromanage them.

Understand Your Mission

Most companies have a mission statement, which is defined as a formal summary of the aims and values of a company, organization, or individual. Whether your focus is on doing what is right for your customers or caring for a patient, the why is essential to your company, and it should be relevant to you and your team.

Understanding your Mission Statement and the "Why" behind it creates a driving culture in your team. What do Steve Jobs (Apple), and Jeff Bezos (Amazon) have in common? A universal message and mission, and by understanding that they drove their companies to new levels. A mission statement that is taken seriously and widely communicated may provide insights into the corporate culture.

The Six Emotional Leadership Styles

Daniel Goleman, Richard Boyatzis, and Annie McKee detailed their Six Emotional Leadership Styles theory in their 2002 book, "Primal Leadership." The approach highlights the strengths and weaknesses of six common styles – Visionary, Coaching, Affiliative, Democratic, Pacesetting, and Commanding. It also shows how each form can affect the emotions of your team members.

It is essential to keep in mind that it is rare for any leader to have just one leadership style. Most leaders will have two or more leadership styles that shine through.

Coercive

The coercive style seeks immediate compliance from employees. As a style that can be linked to that of a dictatorship, it can be summed up with "Do what I tell you." Leaders demand immediate compliance.

Pacesetting

Similar to the coercive style, the pacesetting style should be used sparingly. It is also known as the "do as I do, now" style. Leaders expect excellence and self-direction.

Visionary

In the authoritative style, visionary leaders take a "firm but fair" approach that mobilizes members toward a specific goal. Leaders mobilize people toward a shared vision.

Democratic

The democratic style can be summed up with the question "What do you think?" Focused on getting feedback, leaders can receive valuable ideas and confirmation while building an environment of trust, commitment, and respect. Leaders build consensus through participation.

Affiliative

In this "people come first" style, an affiliative leader praises and nurtures members to cultivate a sense of belonging in an organization. Leaders create emotional bonds and harmony.

Coaching

Some leaders can maximize their workers' effectiveness by acting as a coach instead of a traditional boss. In the "try this" model, leaders focus on the strengths and weaknesses of an employee to improve and encourage him or her along the way. Leaders develop people for the future.

The Five Major Leadership Styles

Before the list of "Six Emotional Leadership Styles," there was a definitive list of five major leadership styles. This list is a combination of leadership styles from that date back to the 1930's to more modern times.

Regardless of the era, they come from, the styles transcend the passage of time and still reflect styles of leadership that can be incorporated into the six emotional leadership styles. Which when you tie to the two together paints a good picture of your overall leadership style.

1. **Bureaucratic leadership**, whose leaders focus on following every rule.

2. **Laissez-faire leadership** is a leadership style that gives their team members a lot of freedom in how the work is accomplished and how their deadlines are set.

3. **Charismatic leadership**, in which leaders inspire enthusiasm in their teams and are energetic in motivating others to move forward.

4. **Servant leadership**, whose leaders focus on meeting the needs of the team.

5. **Transactional leadership**, in which leaders inspire by expecting the best from everyone and themselves.

Things to Avoid

Behind Closed Doors

Do not condemn or demean someone within the company in public or behind closed doors. This will generally demoralize the employee and lower their self-esteem. In the end, it will hurt the efficiency and productivity of the employee.

Make Time

Not making time for your team. It is easy for any leader to focus on all of the tasks they have every day. Make sure you are spending some time or least checking in with your team a few times a day.

Don't Be Too Removed

Being too hands off on any project is a bad thing. While delegating is an integral part of being a leader avoid and micromanaging is a bad thing, you need to find the right balance.

Move On

Misunderstanding your role is a common mistake with most new leaders. Once you move into a leadership role, your responsibilities are very different from those you had before.

Listen To Your Employees

You would think this is a no-brainer but if you look at other managers within your own landscape and pay close attention this is usually a chronic issue in most organizations. Not listening to your employees as often as possible is a common mistake made by managers. By listening to them often you are building loyalty and trust.

Not Being Visible

One of the important things a leader must do on a daily basis is to be visible to your team. It is crucial to reach out to your employees every day. The encounters do not need to be formal and it could just be as simple as seeing how their day is going.

Being visible lets your team know that you are there for them and you acknowledge them. It will keep the morale high through your connections that you are making with them.

2
Servant Leadership

"A leader is best when people barely know he exists when his work is done, his aim fulfilled, they will say: we did it ourselves."

- *Lao Tzu*

THE TERM "SERVANT LEADERSHIP" was first coined by Robert Greenleaf in 1970. Traditional leadership generally involves the exercise of power by one at the "top of the pyramid." By comparison, the servant-leader shares power puts the needs of others first and helps people develop and perform as highly as possible.

Servant leadership turns the power pyramid upside down which puts the typically low-level employees at the top of the pyramid; instead of the people working to serve the leader, the leader exists to help the people.

This model can be a difficult transition for most managers who are used to putting their needs first and are usually driven by success. You must genuinely want to help your employees for this model to be successful. There is nothing more gratifying than to help develop your employees to achieve their goals. Regardless of the organization you work for this leadership style is effective and you can make significant changes in the organization.

Nine Qualities of a Servant Leader

1. **Values Others Opinions** - A servant leader values everyone's opinions and their contributions.

2. **Cultivates an Environment of trust** – A Servant leader does not promote gossiping and does not promote an environment that accepts that.

3. **Develops Leaders** – A servant leader understands the importance of developing others. It is a matter of leading by example and teaching others. Sometimes the leader must not always lead, but instead give up power to allow others to lead so others can learn.

4. **Helps people with life issues** – There is no question that focusing on business is a top priority when working with your employees. However, a servant leader will help their employees with some life issues, such as certain family situations, and seeking to help them with find education for debt concerns.

5. **Encourages Employees** - The corner stone of any servant leader is <u>encouragement</u>. A servant leader also understands to get involved with employees when working on issues. The servant leader will say "Let's go do it" instead of "you."

6. **Sells instead of tells** - A servant leader is the opposite of a dictator. It's a style all about persuading, not commanding.

7. **It's not all about them** - There's a selfless quality about a servant leader. Someone who is thinking only, "How does this benefit me?" is disqualified.

8. **Thinks long-term** - A servant leader is thinking about the next generation, the next leader, and the next opportunity. That means a tradeoff between what's essential today versus tomorrow, and making choices to benefit the future.

9. **Acts with humility** - The leader doesn't wear a title as a way to show who's in charge, doesn't think he is better than everyone else, and acts in a way to care for others. They may pick up the trash or clean up a table. Setting an example of service, the servant leader understands that it is not about the leader, but about others.

Things to Avoid

Multitasking

People often boast about how good they are at multitasking. They think they are getting more done by juggling multiple tasks at once, but studies show that they aren't. When people multitask, their productivity decreases by as much as 40%.

Paying attention to multiple communication media at the same time, such as texting while listening to a colleague, may best be characterized as the "illusion of multitasking." Unlike listening to music and writing a report, which may be accomplished simultaneously, trying to communicate through multiple media channels usually does not result in positive outcomes.

Procrastination

Procrastination is the habit of delaying or putting off doing something that should be done right away. Everyone procrastinates sometimes. But when people procrastinate, they run the risk of jeopardizing their projects—and their reputations.

Micromanaging

While micromanaging it may be necessary for some employees don't let this be your overall management styles. This will only slow you down. There are just so many hours in each work week and your time working each week will start to creep up.

Most employees despise the micromanager. It can damage your relationship with the employee and can come across as if you do not trust them.

Dismissing Other's Ideas

This is generally a bad move, and you should never have your employees feel like you do not value their opinion.

3
Micromanagement

*"An employee's motivation is a direct result of the sum of
interactions with his or her manager."*

- ***Bob Nelson***

Micromanaging has adverse effects on employees and
causes a decrease in productivity. Micromanagement is not
only a lousy leadership style as it has negative impacts on
the organization, but it also has adverse effects on the
employees that work for that organization. Understanding
leadership styles is an essential step in identifying your
strengths and weaknesses. Being a strong leader and
avoiding micromanagement is not only crucial for the
leader in the role it is also critical for the organization as a
whole. Having strong leadership skills is essential for the
employees that work for that organization.

First and foremost, micromanaging has a direct and
negative impact on employee productivity. By not being a
micromanager allows the employee to "fly on their own"
and is found to be 21% more productive than someone who
is not being micromanaged.

Micromanagement impacts the organization as studies have
found that turnover is my higher for the company.
Employee turnover can be 25% higher which in the end
effects the productivity of your employees.

In some cases, micromanagement may increase productivity over the short term, but long-term problems will eventually defeat any short-term gains.

Micromanaging employees has other negative impacts on employees such as, they no longer take risks, creativity dries up, and customer service goes down. The micromanager severely damages the productivity of the organization and, over the long run, may jeopardize the organization's survival.

Key Characteristics of the Micromanager

Watching Too Closely

Micromanagers tend to oversee their employees too closely and spend a lot of time supervising over a project or the daily operations. The need to know specific details of their employee's schedule, plan, meetings, and other work-related conversations.

Difficulty Delegating

Micromanagers have a problem with trusting in their employees to complete a task themselves and will in return end up owning the task.

Consistently Overextending

Micromanagers are consistently overextending themselves and their staff and they will usually take on too many different projects. It is difficult for the micromanager to understand why they are so busy when tasks are itemized it is realized they are trying to do all of the jobs of the organization.

Must Be Right

The micromanager must be right at all costs and they are always looking to place blame on everyone around them but themselves. They will be the first ones to throw their employees right under the bus. This creates a toxic environment and increases the stress levels of the employees ultimately impacting morale.

If you Realize You're a Micromanager

You may now realize that you are a micromanager, and that is ok. The good news is recognizing and accepting that you are one is the first step to correcting it. It is not uncommon for micromanagers change their management styles after learning there are better ways to lead your team.

Let them Fail

In order for most individuals to learn and grow it is important to let them fail. Micromanagers usually hold not only themselves but others to strict standards as they are perfectionists. Let the employee falter and stammer in order to understand why they shouldn't perform the task a certain way. After all, you have learned that along the way at some point and some of the toughest lessons are the ones that are usually not forgotten.

Let Them Come to You

You will want to encourage an open line of communication. It is important to set expectations when a task or project is assigned to have them come to you with any questions or concerns they may have.

Give More Responsibility

Give your employees more responsibility that you feel comfortable with. While this may not be easy to do initially but the more often you do, it will get easier.

Don't Dictate Everything

So now that you are giving out more responsibility it is important that you do not provide a specific roadmap on how to complete a project or task. Allow the employee some freedom to figure out how to complete it on their own. As previously mentioned set expectations but you shouldn't spell it out for them.

Learn to Trust

Most micromanagers have trust issues and they do so because of this. Remember that not everyone can perform the job exactly the way you want it. Take a deeper look at yourself and confront your personal issues with this.

Focus on Management

Perhaps you were the best operator before you moved into your leadership role, and your understanding of the material your employees handle is far superior. It is important to understand that you are now a manager and leader of the group. You need to excel at your new role and focus on being that manager and leader. Let your team perform the tasks they need to and you need to focus on management tasks.

Ways to Combat Being Micromanaged

Don't assume because you are now in a leadership position that you yourself will not be micromanaged. It is not uncommon for managers themselves to be micromanaged by their supervisor. The good news is there are a few ways to combat being micromanaged.

Assess your Own Behavior

Determine if there is specific reason why your supervisor is micromanaging you. Sometimes those micromanaging us have a good reason, evaluate yourself and see if there are certain areas that your supervisor continues to focus on or is constantly bringing up.

Challenge your Supervisor

Talk with your supervisor and address your concern with them, perhaps they can provide you some insight and set expectations on what they expect from you. There is nothing wrong talking about this and seeing if there is a common ground you both can reach.

Frequent Communication

Keeping your supervisor in the loop is a great way to combat being micromanagement. It builds trust between the two of you and shows that you are not trying to go rogue. It also demonstrates your competency when you are staying on tops of the tasks or projects assigned to you.

Anticipate Their Needs

Most micromanagers have triggers that and you can develop a sense on what those are. This will help you expect this type of behavior and will lower your stress. Once you have identified their triggers it will allow you to stay one step ahead of them.

Things to Avoid

Owning Everything

It is important to not own every task or project. You must learn to rely on your staff and make sure you are delegating when needed. If this is a hard habit to break, setup a weekly or biweekly meeting to get brought up to speed on the progress.

Controlling Everything

Understand that you cannot control everything and that
there is no way to predict every situation. Something will
eventually go wrong and it is better to allow the employee
who owns the task or project to attempt to fix it themselves.

Being Overbearing

It is important to step back and let your team members
manage themselves. Do not check in on them hourly and
set some guidelines for yourself. Employees hate nothing
more than to have their boss hovering over them
throughout the day.

Immerse Themselves

Micromanagers have the tendency to immerse themselves
in overseeing the projects of others. They will reason that
they not only need to be involved in this project but
somehow is a reflection of themselves.

Discourage Others

They will feel as though all decisions their employees make
must go through them. The will discourage others to
approach them first instead of making decisions on their
own.

SECTION 2

BEST PRACTICES

Best Practices (Plural Noun) best prac-tices - A procedure that has been shown by research and experience to produce optimal results and that is established or proposed as a standard suitable for widespread adoption

Synonyms: application, exercise, use, operation, implementation, execution;

4
Communication

"I speak to everyone the same way, whether he is the garbage man or the president of the university."

- *Albert Einstein*

DON'T JUST BE A GREAT SPEAKER, be a great communicator. There are few things more important than communication. As a leader, you must make sure you are consistently focused on your communication skill sets as it can be challenging for most leaders. The information you send and receive are not only crucial during a typical day but even more critical during challenging days.

We live in a world where communication has improved dramatically within the past few decades thanks to the advancement of technology. It is not hard to get overwhelmed with all the ways anyone can reach you to you at any given time.

It is essential to keep in mind that mismanaging the way people communicate with you and vice-versa can be a drain on your efficiencies. There a quite few things you can do to keep from getting stressed out and remain an effective leader and be the "great communicator."

In business, poor communication costs money and wastes time. One study found that 14% of each workweek is wasted on poor communication. In contrast, effective communication is an asset for organizations and individuals alike. Effective communication skills, for example, are an asset for job seekers.

Types of Communication

Communication can be categorized into three basic types, including (1) verbal communication, in which you listen to a person to understand meaning; (2) written communication, in which you read meaning; and (3) nonverbal communication, in which you observe a person and infer meaning. Each of these types has its own advantages and disadvantages.

<u>Email</u>

Thomas Jefferson summed up the rules of writing well with this idea: "Don't use two words when one will do." Put another way, half the words can have twice the impact. One of the oldest myths in business is that writing more will make you sound more important, but the opposite is true. Leaders who can communicate simply and clearly project a stronger image than those who write a lot but say nothing.

Stay Current

If staying on top of email is an issue for you it is best to put some time on your calendar if needed for administrative work.
Emails need to be checked every work day, and it is easy to fall behind or even get in the habit of not checking daily.

Like it or not email is just a part of the job and important to stay on top of.

Set an Out of Office

Make sure you have an "Out of Office Message" when you are not in the office. Make sure that the out of office message include the day(s) you are out and also when you are expected to return. Offer an alternate or backup they can call if possible.

Read Twice, Send Once

Prior to send out any email review it at least twice. This will not only help you make sure you are sending out the right message but it will also prevent you from looking foolish.

When Sending Out Mass Emails

When sending out an email to large groups of people it is best to include all employees in the BCC field. By using the BCC field it will prevent employees to send replies to everyone on the email. This will reduce the amount of email clutter, and everyone on the email will appreciate this.

Be detailed, when sending out mass emails. Ensuring that all the important dates, contacts, places and pertinent information will reduce the amount of further questions or concerns people may have.

Desk Phone

Set up your voicemail

This may seem like an obvious one, but I have encountered this one countless times. You can come across as unorganized or as if you don't care if you do not have your voicemail setup.

Professional Voicemail Greeting

Make sure that your voicemail greeting is professional. It is important to make sure you voicemail message uses the appropriate tone, verbiage and it is not too long.

Call Back

Return all calls within a timely fashion; when you receive a voicemail don't procrastinate. If you received a lot of calls prioritize who gets called back first.

Again, Set an Out of Office

Make sure you have an "Out of Office message" on both your desk phone and or cell phone. It is not the responsibility of the caller to know your schedule.

Make sure that the out of office message include the day(s) you are out and also when you are expected to return. Offer an alternate contact or backup contact that they can call if possible.

Cell Phone

Text Messages

Text messages are becoming increasingly more popular as a form of communication for job requests. If possible, I would avoid using this as a primary mode of communication. There are times that we need to tune out the phone calls and texts. While it may be hard to disconnect, sometimes there are times that it is necessary. The other concern is a text could be personal or business and staying focused on work can be difficult if you are receiving a lot of personal text messages.

Set an Out of Office!

I know I sound like a broken record, however, if people are reaching out to you on your cell phone for business, make sure you are also putting an out of office message on your phone when you are on vacation, sick, or on holiday.

Instant Messaging

Use Sparingly

More and more companies are using instant messaging as a form of communicating. While this is a great way to get answers to quick questions, keep in mind that it can rob someone's focus. So use this sparingly.

Communicate Back

If you do not have time to speak with someone at that time, let them know and get back with them when you have more time.

Turn this off or set it to "do not disturb" when you need to concentrate. Someone could potentially reach out to you at any time and break that concentration.

Group Messaging

Use For Urgent Messages

Sometimes emailing urgent messages can be too slow and can be missed by some. This is a great tool to use when communicating urgent messages that need to be sent out.

Create a group for your team as well as for leadership communications. This will help organize mass communications which can be catered to your audience.

Set the rules. This type of communication should be used for urgent issues only not to talk about trivial topics or topics that can wait to be discussed face to face.

One on One Employee Sessions

Perform Monthly 1:1's

Performing one on ones are a great way to get to better under connect with your employees. Make sure you are completing your one on ones with all of your employees each month.

If you have more than 25 employees, perform these quarterly. Otherwise, you find that this is taking up a lot of your time that could probably be focused elsewhere.

Give Them Time

While it is essential to cover the requested questions set forth by your leadership, it is necessary to allow the employee time to speak about whatever is on their mind. As a leader, it is good practice to hold your thoughts and allow the employee to do most of the talking. Do 80% of the listening and 20% of the talking.

Public Speaking

Public speaking is difficult for most people. There are an estimated 87% of all Americans have glossophobia, which is a fear of public speaking. So you are not alone, and most audience speakers understand this and understand the difficulties of public speaking.

Be prepared!

How do you get to Carnegie Hall? Practice, Practice, Practice. If you have a presentation that you need to present, give yourself some time with it, bring it home and practice it behind closed doors. This will allow you to be more comfortable with the content.

Know your Audience

Remember who you are speaking to and tailor the message for them. Try to leave the jargon out of the presentation unless they are knowledgeable on the material.

Be Yourself

Don't try to be anyone else but yourself when speaking in front of an audience. You may not come across as genuine and lose some of the audience.

Tell A Story

Being able to connect to your audience is crucial. Adding a personal touch to your presentation can really have an effect on the material you are presenting as it draws your audience in.

Paperwork

While physical paperwork becomes less due to the advancement of technology and communications, there is still plenty of it in the work environment.

Don't Keep Everything

Avoid the clutter, if a paper communication doesn't require a response from you, skim it, and then toss or file it. If a paper communication requires a response from you, respond immediately, then toss it, file it or shred it.

Stay Organized

Stay organized with the paperwork and keep it in specific folders if you need to retain a physical copy.

If you're too busy to respond right away, put the document in a "Later" file. Be sure to rank the items by priority.

Scan What You Can

If you don't need to keep the physical copy scan it on a copier and keep in organized on your computer.

Shred What You Don't Need

Shred any work documents that you don't need; this will ensure the communication will remain confidential and help out the environment.

Stay up to Date

Go through your documents every so often, say once a quarter to see if the information is still relevant. If you are not sure if you still need it, scan it!

Things to Avoid

Avoid To Many Audiovisuals

When speaking publicly and presenting, it is important to keep the audiovisuals, such as videos, to a minimum.

Having too many breaks during your presentation can cause a disconnect between you are your audience.

Stay Focused

When having conversations with people avoid multitasking. You must be present for the discussion regardless of how menial it may seem.

Pick Up The Phone

When you need a direct answer or something that requires a high level of detail pick up the phone. Sometimes it is just easier, and quicker to pick up the phone and talk about it.

Leave Emotion out of Emails

Emails are great when you need to send out a communication with facts. It can be difficult to convey emotion in emails and when attempted it could easily be misconstrued. If you need to convey a message with emotion it is best to do this verbally.

Don't Email Everything

Oral communication makes more sense when the sender is conveying a sensitive or emotional message, needs feedback immediately, and does not need a permanent record of the conversation.

5
Time Management

"Don't be fooled by the calendar. There are only as many days in the year as you make use of. One man gets only a week's value out of a year while another man gets a full year's value out of a week."

- *Charles Richards*

TIME MANAGEMENT IS VITAL as your calendar is going to start getting filled up. Email. Voicemail. Meetings. Paperwork. Employee Engagement. Projects. Essential requests from multiple people at once. Direct reports who continually ask for help or bring you their problems. There is no question that it is crucial to have strong time management skills.

Time management is all about remaining organized. The more organized you are, the better you can effectively manage time for projects, requests, and your employees. If you can control time better, this can lower your stress levels.

Managing Your Time Effectively

Time management is more than just deciding you'll spend 30 minutes on one task and an hour on another. It is also about organizing your tasks to see what needs to be accomplished through your day and setting priorities.

Manage Your Time Effectively

Clarify Your Goals

You need to first identify your priorities so you can use your time in the best way possible to accomplish them. Without setting priorities you run the risk of putting off important tasks and not meeting deadlines.

Assess how you use your time

It is important track your time and look for ways to improve how you spend it. You should only need to do this occasionally if you find you there is never enough time in the day to accomplish all of your tasks.

By tracking your time over a week's period you can start to identify where your time is being spent and adjust as needed.

Devise a Plan

If you are not already it is important to start creating schedules and to-do lists that map out how you plan to spend your time. This will help you streamline your time management.

Implement Your Plan

Now that you have identified how you are spending your time and have created your to-do lists and schedules you need to hold yourself accountable. By putting your strategy in place and executing your plan it will protect yourself from distractions that can prevent you from executing your plan.

Improve Your Plan

Just like any good plan it is important to understand they are fluid and can change. You need to assess your progress toward achieving your goals and adjust your approach as needed.

Examples of Time Management

"Time Blocking"

Time Blocking is a method that is used by blocking time on your calendar to specific tasks it helps hold yourself accountable. An example of this would be to set time aside to perform admin tasks like email.

If you start finding some tasks more difficult to accomplish then set time aside for that task and close your door over or put some headsets on.

Have a Task List

Capture the tasks and activities you must do on a list and update it regularly during the day. Revisit this list frequently and add new items as soon as they appear. Make sure your list gives you a quick overview of everything that's urgent and important, and remember to include strategic and relationship-building activities as well as operational tasks.

Minimize Interruptions

The more uninterrupted time you get during the day to work on essential tasks, the more effective you will be.

Identify the activities that tend to disrupt your work, and find a solution. For example, avoid checking emails and answering the phone when you're in the middle of something important.

Delegate

If you are to add maximum value, you must learn to delegate. This will help you create space to concentrate on the big picture and the strategic aspects of your top agendas of the day.

Be Organized

This might sound like another obvious one, however, being organized can be a constant struggle for some new leaders. The more organized you are, the better your stress levels will be, and you'll have more control over time management.

Identify Your Time Management Style

Think about your time management style by reflecting on some key areas. It is important to understand your time management style and determine where you need to improve.

First, you will need to identify what your motivation is for managing your time. For an example, perhaps you find you are spending too much time at your desk, or are simply working too many hours during the week, you need to find out what your motivation is to improve your time management.

You will also need to identify what your current time management abilities are. By identifying your strengths and weaknesses you can you start to build your base.

Your biggest time management challenges need to be identified as well. It is important to determine your challenges in order to overcome them.

There are certain tasks that can that give you energy—and those that can sap it. While some tasks are unavoidable perhaps you need to look at your approach to them and change how you handle them.

We are all different and there are some times of day when you're most and least focused. For some it is early in the day while others it is midday. Once you identify what time of the day you have the most energy, start to pile on the tasks during those times.

Family Comes First!

We put all this emphasis on time-management at work and being able to perform your job efficiently, remember however that family always comes first and if you need to reschedule something for your family (emergency, important family event, etc.) Reschedule!

Things to Avoid

Delegating To The Wrong Person

Delegating work will save you hours if you are empowering to the right people. Appointing work to the wrong person could end up increasing the workload if it is not done correctly. Ensure you are delegating to an individual with the right skillsets.

Don't Take On Too Much

Don't take on too much responsibility. If you are asked to take on additional work and say yes to everyone, then you run the risk of taking on too much. While it may be hard, sometimes you have to say "no."

Keep A To-Do List

Failing to keep a to-do list is a significant time management mistake. With all of the tasks you have to do daily, it can be challenging to keep it straight. The last thing you need is to remember something you forgot to do on your way home. It can ruin your night.

Today, Not Tomorrow

Don't procrastinate, do what you can today and not tomorrow. The more you procrastinate the more work piles up and increases your stress levels. If you need to stay late and wrap up your work.

6
Meetings

"The number of meetings I've been in – people would be shocked. But that's how you gain experience, how you can gain knowledge, being in meetings and participating. You learn and grow."

- *Tiger Woods*

OH THE DREADED MEETINGS! Some days/weeks can be filled with them. The more you move up that corporate ladder, it is inevitable that you will have more and more meetings. If you are not hosting the meeting, it is essential that you are engaged. Whether it is a meeting that is on the phone, a WebEx or at a physical location you must remain engaged at all times.

When I first made my transition into a management role, I was surprised by the number of meetings that I needed to attend. The weekly project meetings, monthly team meetings the quarterly updates, biannual updates and annual updates. Anyone who has been part of a team knows that it involves team meetings. While few individuals relish the idea of meetings, they serve an important function in terms of information sharing and decision making. They are also an important social function that can help build team cohesion and coordinate task functions.

Teleconference or Web Conferencing

Make sure you are always announcing yourself when speaking in large groups on a teleconference. Not everyone knows your voice and it can get very confusing for all parties when you do not announce yourself.

Remember to put yourself on mute. This can avoid any background noise that the rest of the audience can hear. Also, it can prevent any awkward conversations you may be having while you are waiting for the meeting to being.

Arrive early if possible; this will allow you to prepare for the meeting if needed.

When Hosting a Meeting

Before the Meeting

Decide who should be at the meeting and only invite those people. The more people who attend a meeting, the less each person will participate, so there should be a reason why each person is invited to the meeting. Consider who should absolutely be there and limit your invitation to those individuals.

Have an agenda! This will help keep the meeting stay on the topic. An agenda will inform those invited about the purpose of a meeting. It also helps organize the flow of the meeting and keep the team on track.

Send a reminder prior to the meeting. Reminding everyone of the purpose, time, and location of a meeting helps everyone prepare themselves. If a team meets only to find that there is no reason for the meeting because members haven't completed their agreed-upon tasks, team performance or morale can be negatively impacted

During and After the Meeting

Make sure that someone is taking meeting minutes and writing down essential keynotes, such as dates, names, projects, etc. If no can be assigned, then the host should do their best to take critical notes and send them out to those that have attended after the meeting is over.

If you are the host, it is important to start on time and to be mindful of other people's time. Waiting for members who are running late only punishes those who are on time and reinforces the idea that it's okay to be late.

Announce who the key stakeholders on the call. There is no need to go into high detail, just their name, title is usually enough.

When the meeting veers off topic as the host, it is essential to set the meeting back in the right direction. Veering off from the agenda communicates to members that the agenda is not important. It also makes it difficult for others to keep track of where you are in the meeting.

Summarize the meeting with action items. Be sure to clarify team member roles moving forward. If individuals' tasks are not clear, chances are that role confusion will arise later. There should be clear notes from the meeting regarding who is responsible for each action item and the time frames associated with next steps.

End the meeting on time. This is vitally important, as it shows that you respect everyone's time and are organized. If another meeting is needed to follow up, schedule it later, but don't let the meeting run over.

Things to Avoid

Is the Meeting Needed?

Leaders should do a number of things prior to a meeting to make it more effective, the first being to make sure the meeting is even needed. If the meeting is primarily informational in nature, ask yourself if it is imperative that the group fully understands the information and if future decisions will be built upon this information. If so, a meeting may be needed. If not, perhaps simply communicating with everyone in a written format will save valuable time.

Give the Pen a Break

It is great that you are taking notes however taking too many notes can leave you unengaged in the meeting. Find a balance between taking notes when needed and staying engaged in the meeting.

Don't get distracted... Focus!

It is crucial to remain focused and engaged in the meeting. These days there are so many devices that can rob us of our focus, like our phone or computer.

Try to leave your computer behind; It is common for leaders to discourage flat out bringing a laptop to a meeting.

Turn your phone off or over. If possible disconnect from your phone as well. This is just another tool to rob you from your focus.

Back to Back Meetings

It is good to have at least 10-15 mins in between meeting to reflect on the meeting that was just had and collect your thoughts. So it is important to avoid scheduling back to back meetings if you can.

While avoiding meetings back to back is not always possible if anything else, be mindful to limit this is possible.

If you are setting a meeting and forego the last 10 minutes of the meeting set up the meeting for 50-minute intervals instead of the hour. Everyone at the meeting with a busy schedule will appreciate it.

Watch out for Double Booking

If this is unavoidable make sure you set up a proxy in your place in one of the meetings and try to get your proxy up to speed as best you can.

Not Being Prepared

Not being prepared is just not acceptable, if you are invited to a meeting and expectations are set, do not go to the meeting unprepared.

Mute your Cell Phone

If you cannot turn your cell phone off mute it. If you must take a call and are in a physical meeting then leave the meeting that you are in and taking the phone call is proper etiquette. It is bad form to take the call in the room when a meeting is going on.

Don't Announce Yourself When arriving Late

There is no need to announce yourself when you are late for a meeting; it will most likely interrupt the speaker and throw off the pace of the meeting.

SECTION 3

Employee Interaction

Employee (Noun) em-ploy-ee - A person employed for wages or salary, especially at nonexecutive level.

Synonyms: worker, working man/woman, member of staff, staffer, blue-collar worker, white-collar worker, laborer, workingman, hand, hired hand, wage earner; personnel, staff, workforce;

7
Hiring/Interviewing

"Time spent hiring is time well spent."

- ***Robert Half***

HIRING AND INTERVIEWING is another crucial skillset that you must continuously improve. Having a right fit for your team is extremely important and having someone that is toxic could spread like cancer to the rest of the team. I cannot emphasize the importance of spending time on the hiring process.

It is essential to put some focus on becoming a good interviewer. Ensuring that you are an excellent interviewer guarantees when you interview someone the experience is comfortable for both you and the interviewee.

Hiring/Interviewing

Hiring Panel

Practice

The more interviewing opportunities, the better, try to get involved in as many interviews as possible. It is not uncommon to sit on the hiring panel for other departments, so if you see an opportunity, grab it.

Use The Same Questions

Be consistent with questioning when interviewing multiple candidates. This will ensure how each candidate responds to the same questions.

Identify the Questions

There are great interview questions and other recommendations when performing an interview. It is essential to do some research to find some the right interview questions that would be helpful to practice.

Use an Interview Grid

When interviewing multiple potential employees, it is good to use an interview grid. An interview grid allows you to rate the interviewee during the interview process. This is helpful only to identify or "grade" the employee's strengths and weaknesses. It could be used whether you are on a panel or interviewing one on one.

Know the Candidates

It is important to make sure you thoroughly go through the candidates resumes prior to interviewing them. Resumes are a great way to look at their background information and give you an opportunity to cross exam them based on the information that they have provided.

Nonverbal Communication

Research shows that nonverbal cues can also affect whether you get a candidate gets a job. Judges examining videotapes of actual applicants were able to assess the social skills of job candidates with the sound turned off. They watched the rate of gesturing, time spent talking, and the formality of dress to determine which candidates would be the most successful socially on the job. For this reason, it is important to consider how we appear in business as well as what we say. The muscles of our faces convey our emotions, so we can send a silent message without saying a word.

Ask Behavioral Based Questions

Depending on the job you are interviewing for this may or may not seem obvious. For example, if this is for a Human Resource position it only makes sense to ask behavioral questions. However, if this is for a technical job, it may be more difficult to understand why this is needed.

Asking questions for problem-solving skills or integrity questions can provide insight on the potential employee that you may have otherwise looked over during the interview process and peel the surface back a bit to see if they may or may not get along with your team.

- Behavioral Based Question Example #1 - **Problem Solving:** Tell me about an experience in which you turned a problem into a success.

- Behavioral Based Question Example #2 – **Integrity:** When was the last time you 'broke the rules?' What was the situation and what did you do?

Setup Back to Back Interviews

This will help with consistency and tone when asking questions. It will also help with the flow of the meeting. Identify who will start with the questions and the order of who will go next.

<u>Peer Panels</u>

This is a great way to get feedback from your team for a potential hire. It also makes them feel like they are more involved in the process.

Ensure that the employees that you are going to perform the interview are adequately trained or coached. This can be uncomfortable for all parties if they are not trained on interview questions.

Onboarding

Not having a smooth onboarding is a major complaint from most new employees and can be a painful experience for most new employees. Onboarding is a crucial area needed to be focused on for any new employees. So it is essential for you to have a plan!

Many organizations, take a more structured and systematic approach to new employee onboarding, while others follow a "sink or swim" approach in which new employees struggle to figure out what is expected of them and what the norms are.

Have a Program

An orientation program is important, because it has a role in making new employees feel welcome in addition to imparting information that may help them to be successful in their new jobs. Many large organizations have formal orientation programs consisting of lectures, videotapes, and written material, while some may follow more unusual approaches.

Formal orientation programs are helpful in teaching employees about the goals and history of the company, as well as communicating the power structure. Moreover, these programs may also help with a new employee's integration into the team.

Announcement

You've just hired this talented person for your team -- don't keep it quiet! Spread the word around, send out an email, get the word out! This will not only ensure that everyone is expecting a new co-worker, it will promote a positive and transparent environment.

Before Day 1

Keep in regular contact with your new hire. Send any paperwork that can be completed in advance so as not to slow down that first day.

Jargon busting

I've yet to find a company that doesn't have its language and jargon. Whether it's those pesky acronyms that people use (but can't always explain!)

Rules of engagement

Whether this is the new hire's first job or he or she has worked in the industry a long time, you *must* spend time explaining the rules of engagement, otherwise known as the corporate and team etiquette that ensures success.

Sweat the Small Stuff

Don't underestimate the impact of not addressing the small stuff. Which number is needed to dial an outside line? How do you use the photocopier? Where are the restrooms? Where is the coffee machine? When are lunch breaks taken? It's the little things that can be the most frustrating when we are new to a team and are trying to be at our best.

Provide A Mentor

Mentors can be crucial to helping new employees adjust by teaching them the ins and outs of their jobs and how the company really operates. A mentor is a trusted person who provides an employee with advice and support regarding career-related matters. Although a mentor can be any employee or manager who has insights that are valuable to the new employee, mentors tend to be relatively more experienced than their protégés.

Things to Avoid

Warm Bodies

Do not hire a "warm body." Sometimes it can be difficult to fill a spot, do not hire someone to fill the spot. Make sure they are the right fit for the job and find someone that will work well with the team.

Avoid Large Hiring Panels

Don't have huge panels of six or more people; this can be very intimidating to even the most skilled interviewee. Break down into smaller groups if possible

Marathon Interviews

Avoid the marathon interviews; Interviews do not need to exceed more than 60 minutes per session. Focus on the areas you would like to cover and if you find yourself continually going over 60 minutes to evaluate the questions and "trim the fat."

8
Evaluating Team Members

"Only the guy who isn't rowing has time to rock the boat."

- **Jean-Paul Sartre**

EVALUATING TEAM MEMBERS is an area that can often be overlooked or is an area where not enough emphasis is put on it. It is crucial that you feel comfortable evaluating your team. You need to make sure that they are meeting expectations and that they are held accountable.

It is crucial that as a leader you are identifying strengths and weaknesses in the group. This will not only help you start to focus on certain individuals or teams to improve their weaknesses it will also help you leverage the strengths.

Most employees also want to receive feedback to ensure that they are doing a good job as well as help them grow and improve. Engaged employees care about their work and their company, and that begins with proper evaluation and giving appropriate feedback. By working closely and communicating with your team members, it also ensures that you have a good pulse and remain in tune with their needs and concerns.

Employee engagement and motivation varies depending on the individual. It is important to identify why some employees choose to count the hours, while others pursue excellence. Job performance is the result of three factors, which are, motivation, ability and environment.

Motivation is defined as the desire to achieve a goal or a certain performance level, leading to goal-directed behavior. Ability—or having the skills and knowledge required to perform the job—is also important and is sometimes the key determinant of effectiveness. Finally, environmental factors such as having the resources, information, and support one needs to perform well are critical to determine performance.

Why care about Employee Engagement?

Some of the Benefits of Engaged Employees:

- Engaged employees perform 20% better than non-committed employees. You will find that a team that is engaged is more productive.

- Engaged employees are 87% more likely to stay with the organization. Company loyalty will also help with new hires as the culture is a positive one which is ultimately spread your employees.

- While it is important that all employees take some time off for themselves, engaged employees have 44% lower rates of absenteeism.

- No one likes working with someone that has a bad attitude. Engaged employees have on average 5% higher customer satisfaction rating than those that are not engaged.

- Organizations have found that engaged employees are also 10% higher profitability.

Engaged Employees Lead to:

- Overall increased work performance for both individuals and for teams.

- Increased employee retention, as engaged employees are less likely to leave the organization.

- Improved business outcomes, which meet the expectations of the leadership of the organization but also their customers.

Performing Monthly Rounding

Performing 1:1 is crucial to getting a deeper understanding of the individual and help you build trust between the two of you. This is a great time to sit down and get to know your employees. This shouldn't be treated as a 15 minute conversation, you should take this seriously and make it meaningful.

Do not treat as just something that you need to check off on your ever-growing list of things to do. This is one of the more crucial times that you will spend with your employees.

Evaluating Performance and Potential

- Be objective, specific, and reward accomplishment. Identify areas of needed growth or at least how they can make a good performance great.

- Do your best to provide information from first-hand knowledge.

- Engage high performers in conversation regarding their performance

- Align rewards and recognition to goal achievement and organizational priorities. For example; don't punish good performers by giving them more work. Don't reward poor performers by removing work.

Providing Feedback

When to Provide Feedback

It is important to identify when good work is performed. It is good habit as a leader to provide positive feedback.

When a problem is affecting important outcomes, you must set expectations and then provide feedback on the work.

This will ensure the work being performed stays on the defined track.

How to Provide Feedback

Feedback can be formal like a performance review or informal like a watercooler conversation. This will depend on the type of feedback, how crucial the feedback is and the timeliness of the feedback. Informal feedback is usually ongoing, in the moment advice outside of formal performance reviews.

When providing feedback you need to make sure that you are specific, relevant/balanced, and prompt. The employee must understand how critical the feedback is.

Feedback should be proactive and constructive. The employee should not feel like the feedback is an attack on their work.

Providing Positive Feedback

Be specific about what the action was taken on the work that was performed.

Discuss the impacts with the employee on the department, team, goals, etc. Make sure to tie the feedback to the mission and values whenever possible.

Be prompt about giving positive feedback. Do not wait too long when discussing feedback with the employee or team.

Thank and recognize the team and employees for their excellent work. This can be done one on one or during a group meeting.

Providing Feedback for Improvement

It is important to set expectations, you need to make sure that you are describing the behavior or action that needs to be improved upon.

Describe the impact of the behavior or action has had on the team, the organization, or the project. This is not an attempt to shame the employee but it is important they understand what impacts it had.

Indicate the desired change and manage expectations with the employee. By setting expectations it will further reinforce with the employee the desire for them to succeed.

When needed coach or have them coached by a subject matter expert. It is important to understand what the employee's needs are. Ask questions like – "How can I help you?" and "What can we do for you.....?"

Close the Loop by setting the expectations again for the desired behavior – "Let me clarify my expectation." It is essential to set expectations and encourage employees to think outside of the box and if they are unsure about next steps to come and speak with you.

Things to Avoid

Don't Wait

Don't wait until the last minute to perform a performance review with an employee. You may feel rushed and feel the pressure to get it done. The employee deserves more than something you just threw together.

Provide Insightful Information

Don't have a 10-15 minute performance or evaluation review. This is another example of just not being prepared and not putting any detail into the report.

Be Honest

Not giving negative feedback is more common than you may think. Giving negative feedback is the only way for the employee to know that there is an issue with their performance.

Focus On The Entire Evaluation Period

Using recent behavior as the primary focus of the evaluation instead of the entire performance period should be avoided. It is essential to keep in mind the evaluations usually span over an extended period instead of just what happened last week.

It's Never Personal

Providing feedback should be personal, and it should come directly from you. You should avoid providing feedback from another employee unless you have it in writing.

Address Issues As Needed

Don't let issues pile up and wait for a scheduled evaluation. If there is an issue that is being repeated by the employee or there are multiple concerns do not wait for the evaluation, address your concerns immediately.

9
Team Management

"If everyone is moving forward together, then success takes care of itself."

-   Henry Ford

WITH ANY TEAM DYNAMIC, it is essential to make sure you empower them, communicate well and are setting expectations for the team. Your ability to coordinate and administer a group of individuals is crucial in most management positions. Creating a positive workplace can take any negative perceptions and turn them into a better work environment for everyone.

Getting to know your team is critical and making time for them will motivate your staff when enthusiasm may be lacking. By continuing to evaluate whether they feel valued by you and the company will allow you to make adjustments as needed. Developing your team is a never-ending ongoing process and one that is necessary and time well spent by any leader.

Effective teams give companies a significant competitive advantage. In a high-functioning team, the sum is truly greater than its parts. Team members not only benefit from each other's diverse experiences and perspectives but also stimulate each other's creativity. The aim and purpose of a team is to perform, get results, and achieve victory in the workplace. The best managers are those who can gather together a group of individuals and mold them into an effective team.

Stages of Group Development

American organizational psychologist Bruce Tuckman (1965) presented a well-known model of group development that is still widely used today. Based on his observations of group behavior in a variety of settings, he proposed a four-stage map of group evolution—also known as the forming-storming-norming-performing model. He later enhanced the model by adding a fifth and final stage—the adjourning phase.

According to this theory, in order to successfully facilitate a group, the leader needs to move through various leadership styles over time. Generally, this is accomplished by first being more directive, eventually serving as a coach, and later, once the group is able to assume more power and responsibility for itself, shifting to a delegator role. While research has not confirmed that this is descriptive of how groups progress, knowing and following these steps can help groups be more effective. For example, groups that do not go through the storming phase early on will often return to this stage toward the end of the group process to address unresolved issues.

Forming

In the forming stage, the group comes together for the first time. The members may already know each other or they may be total strangers. In either case, there is a level of formality, some anxiety, and a degree of guardedness as group members are not sure how they will fit into the group or how work will be conducted. "Will I be accepted? What will my role be? Who has the power in this group?"— These are some of the questions participants think about during this stage of group formation. Because of the large amount of uncertainty, members tend to be polite, conflict avoidant, and observant. They are trying to figure out the "rules of the game" without being too vulnerable. The leadership style during this phase should be a coordinator.

Storming

Once group members feel sufficiently safe and included, they tend to enter the storming phase. Participants focus less on keeping their guard up as they shed social facades, becoming more authentic and more argumentative. Group members begin to explore their power and influence, and they often stake out their territory by differentiating themselves from the other group members rather than seeking common ground. Discussions can become heated as participants raise contending points of view and values or argue over how tasks should be done and who is assigned to them. It is not unusual for group members to become defensive, competitive, or jealous. Group members may even take sides or begin to form cliques within the group. The leadership style during this phase should be delegator.

Norming

Group members often feel relief at the norming stage, wherein they are much more committed to each other and the group's goal. Group members feel energized and are now ready to get to work. Finding themselves more cohesive and cooperative, participants find it easy to establish their own ground rules (or *norms*) and define their operating procedures and goals. The group tends to make big decisions, while subgroups or individuals handle the smaller decisions. Hopefully, at this point the group members are more open and respectful toward each other, and members ask each other for both help and feedback. The leadership style during this phase should be directive.

Performing

Galvanized by a sense of shared vision and a feeling of unity, the group is ready to go into high gear. Members are more interdependent, individuality and differences are respected, and group members feel themselves to be part of a greater entity. At the performing stage, participants are not only getting the work done, but they also pay greater attention to *how* they are doing it. The leadership style during this phase should be a coach.

Adjourning

Many groups or teams formed in a business context are project oriented and therefore are temporary in nature. Alternatively, a working group may dissolve due to organizational restructuring. Just as when we graduate from school or leave home for the first time, these endings can be bittersweet, with group members feeling a combination of victory, grief, and insecurity about what is coming next. For those who like routine and bond closely with fellow group members, this transition can be particularly challenging. Group leaders and members alike should be sensitive to handling these endings respectfully and compassionately. An ideal way to close a group is to set aside time to debrief ("How did it all go? What did we learn?"), acknowledge each other, and celebrate a job well done.

Identify Team Roles

It has been identified over there years that there are ten key roles that individuals can take on when working in a group dynamic. It is important for leaders to identify and adapt the roles that the employees are taking on. These roles are core values and behaviors of the employee and it is not uncommon for an employee to take on more than one team role.

Ineffective leaders might identify an employee with a specific social role and continue to engage the employee with no improvement. This is why it is important to identify the social roles the employee takes on and is the right person for the right job.

The ten roles are broken down into three different types of roles. These are task roles, social roles and boundary-spanning roles. Team leadership is effective when leaders are able to adapt the roles they are contributing or ask others to contribute to fit what the team needs given its stage and the tasks at hand.

Task Roles

1. The contractor role includes behaviors that serve to organize the team's work, including creating team timelines, production schedules, and task sequences.

2. The creator role deals mostly with changes in the team's task process structure, such as reframing the team goals and looking at their context.

3. The contributor role is important, because it brings information and expertise to the team.

4. The completer role is also important, as it transforms ideas into action. Behaviors associated with this role include following up on tasks, such as gathering needed background information or summarizing the team's ideas into reports.

5. The critic role includes "devil's advocate" behaviors that go against the assumptions being made by the team.

Social Roles

1. The cooperator is a proactive role that includes supporting those with expertise related to the team's goals.

2. The communicator role includes behaviors that are targeted at collaboration, such as practicing good listening skills and appropriately using humor to

defuse tense situations. Having a good communicator helps the team to feel more open to sharing ideas.

3. The calibrator role is an important one that serves to keep the team on track in terms of suggesting any needed changes to the team's process. This role includes initiating discussions about potential team problems like power struggles or other tensions.

Boundary Spanning Roles

1. The consul role includes gathering information from the larger organization and informing those within the organization about team activities, goals, and successes. Often, the consul role is filled by team managers or leaders.

2. The coordinator role includes interfacing with others within the organization so that the team's efforts are in line with other individuals and teams within the organization.

Foster Trust

Everything about managing your team well depends on earning others' trust in you. If your team is confident that you'll do the right thing as their leader, they will accept your authority and guidance.

When you become a manager, competency is no longer enough—you need to earn people's trust. You have already got to this level, so you were put into leadership because you are known to be a competent employee. Learn the factors that contribute to building trusting relationships.

When Teams Trust Their Leaders

Team will work better through any disagreements that inevitably arise. Disagreements are not abnormal in any team, not everyone can agree at all times. What matters is how you move pass them.

The team members work harder both individually and as a team if they trust their leader.

Employees will stay with an organization longer and they will be more loyal.

Team members will contribute better ideas and more often as they are not afraid to speak up. Leaders will create a positive culture for their employees to feel comfortable to express themselves.

Building Trust Between Members

Trust between members is one of the essential elements of a capable team. When team members trust each other, they are more productive.

Host an off-site Team Meetings

Convene your entire team, including remote members. Time spent together outside the office creates opportunities for team members to get to know one another on a personal level.

Hold Team Lunches

Encourage casual conversation for a half-hour. Prompt team members to reveal a little bit about themselves—their upbringing, families, hobbies, travels.

Add a Personal Touch to Meetings

At the beginning of a meeting, ask each member—those in the room and those joining virtually—to give a brief personal or professional update. Building relationships before the meeting begins, improves communication going forward.

Build Team Cohesiveness

Have team members take a personality test, such as Myers-Briggs, and share the results with the group. Being aware of each other's personality styles helps people feel more comfortable airing conflicts and collaborating.

The fundamental factors affecting group cohesion include the following:

- **Similarity**: The more similar group members are in terms of age, sex, education, skills, attitudes, values, and beliefs, the more likely the group will bond.

- **Stability**: The longer a group stays together, the more cohesive it becomes.

- **Size**: Smaller groups tend to have higher levels of cohesion.

- **Support**: When group members receive coaching and are encouraged to support their fellow team members, group identity is strengthened.

- **Satisfaction**: Cohesion is correlated with how pleased group members are with each other's performance, behavior, and conformity to group norms.

Strengthen Team Identity

Team identity—team members' sense that they share a bond and a purpose are <u>critical for high performance</u>. This ability to bring people together around a common mission.

Benefits of a Team with a Strong Identity

- Teams with a strong identity have a greater willingness to collaborate with each other. The strong the collaboration a team has the more productive they are.

- Teams will feel more comfortable sharing information with each other as they have a better understanding of their peers' roles. They also understand that knowledge should not be used as power.

- Teams will display an increased effort and commitment to each other.

- Joint decision making will be displayed and the team will not feel uncomfortable speaking with each other in group settings.

- Prioritizing team goals ahead of personal goals will be apparent as the team works toward common goals and sets personal goals aside.

Causes of Weak Team Identity

New Teams

It's natural for new teams to suffer from some lack of identity. It is important to not only understand that but make sure that you are focusing on this for new teams. Try to bring the team together as often as possible and create an environment where they all can feel comfortable to communicate with each other.

New Team Members

When new members join the team after the work has begun, team identity can suffer if the newcomers are disruptive or made to feel like outsiders.

The Diversity of Members

Differing assumptions, cultural backgrounds, and ways of working and thinking can lead to misunderstandings or tensions among members.

Lack of a Shared Sense of Purpose

Without a clear and compelling reason for working together, the individuals who make up a team are likely to put their interests above those of the group.

Rally Your Team

From time to time you need to rally your team up to accomplish a task, whether that is a project or just dealing with a heavy operational workload.

- Include everyone, make sure that every able individual is present to assist. This helps with team cohesiveness.

- The critical thing when "rallying the troops" is to make sure that your attitude always remains positive.

- Make sure that you have a clear message and also that your directives are understood by the employees.

- Assign a team leader as needed. When delegating work out make sure that you have identified an owner.

- Provide small incentives when you can. Offer an outing to lunch or bring in breakfast or even order a pizza when the task is complete or during the event.

Things to Avoid

Find Your Balance

Not checking in often enough is the flip side to micromanaging. Having an independent team is excellent, but they still need to hear from their manager from time to time. Visit in on them at least once or twice a day.

Using Email Too Much

Relying on email too much for correspondents is also an issue. While most communications can get put into email, there are some that are best done in person. Set up a meeting with your team and get some good old-fashioned face time in.

Treat Everyone the Same

You need to treat all employees equally. While this seems like another no-brainer, you must make sure they all receive the same equal treatment. This can cause discord in your environment and also create unnecessary employee turnover.

Don't Bully

As a leader, you can intimidate others even if you do not mean it. This is another situation where you want to remember your audience. This is taken very seriously and you could lose your job over this.

Avoid Taboo Subjects

As a manager and leader you must also make sure that you are curbing discussions surrounding race, religion, and politics. Remind your team that these topics are not meant for the workplace. These topics typically make people feel uncomfortable. Also as a leader you should not be using your position as way to get up on your soapbox and spark debates.

Building Walls

There is such a thing as having a team that is too cohesive. The more strongly members identify with the group, the easier it is to see outsiders as inferior or even (in extreme cases) as enemies. This form of prejudice can have a downward spiral effect. It is important to ensure your team keeps this in check and keeps an open mind.

10
Managing Difficult Employees

"One bad apple can spoil the bunch."

-   *Unknown*

THERE IS ONE IS EVERY GROUP, an employee that can be difficult to manage. When you first start working with a new team, this employee may not be easy to recognize, however, once you start working with your team more it is easy to spot one.

Difficult employees that exhibit lousy behavior can impact your team in many ways. Difficult employees affect morale, productivity and customer service satisfaction and overall have a negative impact on the organization.

Depending on the behavior that is exhibited by the employee the actions that can be taken against them span from education to legal action. Identifying and correcting the bad behavior in employees needs to be taken very seriously by their manager. As a leader, it is your responsibility to ensure that your team's wellbeing, productivity, and performance is protected.

Difficult Employee Types

There are quite a few different employee behavioral types which can be broken down and identified easily once you understand what you are looking for. Each style of employee that is listed below can have a negative impact on the team in their own way. Once you had identified it is important to focus in on the employee and manage expectations.

The Bully

This employee style is someone that is always being overcritical of others work and directly disagrees with their manager's expectations. They usually can and does do everything in their power to deter the team from reaching their objectives or at the very least slows the team down.

This employee style is toxic to the team and while constructive criticism should be welcomed this individual usually crosses a line. Identifying this employee style is generally very easy to spot, and if the employee cannot correct this after bringing this to their attention, you need to start considering moving them out of the organization.

The Procrastinator

With all of the work that needs to get done on a daily basis, it is not uncommon to get behind from time to time. However, this employee is usually always behind in their work and is continually requiring to be micromanaged. Once identified make sure that you are managing expectations and holding them accountable when tasks or projects are not met.

The Spotlight Seeker

The spotlight seeker is always finding ways to take credit for other employees work. The attention always needs to be on them. This employee style can be a morale killer for other employees if not identified. It is essential to understand what the employees own when they are working as a team to achieve a goal or complete a project.

The Gossip

Some employees love to spread rumors and not only be a part of gossiping they usually are the ringleaders in most cases. There really is no place for this in any work environment and can cause collateral damage to the team and to you if you do not correct this. When this identified bring this to the attention of the employee and make sure they understand that this is not acceptable.

The Rebel

It can be stressful enough when a situation at work arises, and you need to delegate an owner, and when you approach an employee, they indicate that it is not their job. Perhaps they are even to able to quote their job description.

It is most likely that the employee is disengaged and this needs to be corrected as soon as possible. One way to combat this is to manage expectations for specific situations. It is essential to make sure that the employee understands that certain circumstances warrant requests that may not be in their job descriptions. Job descriptions are more like a guideline and cannot list all the expectations of the company in a few pages.

The Jaded

These types of employees feel that they have given all they can to the company but didn't get anything in return for all of their hard work. The jaded employee is not afraid to let everyone know this and can be very vocal about how the company did not do right by them. This type of employee can be toxic to the environment and may try to have other employees jump on the bandwagon.

If the employee is still engaged then one way to overcome this is to start to recognize the hard work they are doing. However, if they are getting up on their soapbox and are badmouthing the company you need to make sure you bring them in your office and explain that this is not tolerated at your company or at any other.

The Whiner

You are almost guaranteed to have one of these employee styles in your team at one point in your career. While some complaints are justified, this employee has to have something or someone to complain about constantly. This can be very frustrating to deal with as a manager as it is critical to listen to your employees but can be challenging to correct.

It is important to remember that if they are complaining to you about something or someone, then they are most likely complaining to the rest of the team about this issue as well. This employee style can take a positive work environment and turn it into a negative one. This is one employee style that reminds us why it is good to work closely with your team.

The Runaway

This is an employee that is never around when you need them. The employee either disappears physically or is not present mentally. Some topics may and can be uninteresting at times during work. However, this is just not acceptable. Bring this to the employee's attention behind closed doors as soon as you notice this.

The Hot Head

This employee has a temper problem and has difficulty controlling their emotions. Some employers allow this type of employee, however, overreacting in the workplace is just not acceptable. They usually have the tendency to intimidate others and have no problem verbally attacking those that offended them.

While it is not that uncommon for some employees to lose their cool it is the repeat offenders that need to be identified. If you notice a trend, it is essential to address this with them and manage expectations. If they are unwilling to listen or seek out support to correct this behavior it is best to move them out of the organization.

The Super Competitor

There is nothing wrong with healthy competition however you will occasionally encounter the super competitor. They usually take the competition to the next level and can cause tension on the team.

This can also cause undue stress on the other workers during team projects. This is another situation that you need to address head-on with the employee. This is very much a tightrope act as the last thing you want to do to take the wind out of their sails.

The Blamer

While it is crucial for some issues or problems to be identified, this employee is usually the first to point fingers. Not only are they continually shifting responsibility, they never taking ownership of an issue or acknowledge that they have made a wrong decision.

The best approach for rectifying this behavior is to approach the employee head one. Sometimes you need to pick your battles, but if the issue is with the employee, they need to understand the mistakes that were made. Making sure they are held accountable is essential.

The Joker

It is always good to bring a bit of levity to most environments however some employees take this above and beyond and feel like their primary function is to entertain the team. This can be counterproductive as it can distract others from doing their duties. Ensure this employee is keeping this in check and ask them to find a balance.

Things to Avoid

Don't Wait

Anytime you see a behavior that needs to be corrected, you need to focus on fixing that behavior as quickly as possible. If you wait too long the damage to the team could be too great and harder to correct the team's course.

Don't Give Up

Working with an employee to correct a bad behavior can take time. It can be frustrating when lousy employee behavior is not fixed in a timely fashion. If you have tried to adjust the bad behavior with the employee and it does not get corrected the first go around, try a different method to fix it. It may take a few attempts to alter the bad behavior that was exhibited by the employee.

Avoiding The Issue

Not taking any action is the worst thing a manager and a leader can do. Never ignore the issue, this will show your team that you are a leader that does not care about their environment and also a leader that does not take action.

Another message you may send to the team is that the bad behavior is acceptable in the workplace. By not taking action to attempt to correct the bad behavior could also send your team into a tailspin which could be difficult to recover from.

11
Dealing with Employee Conflict

"Don't ever take down a fence until you know why it was put up."

- *Robert Frost*

IT HAPPENS IN GROUPS BOTH BIG AND SMALL, and it is very common to have to deal with employees that do not get along. It could be caused by a long list of things from personalities to lifestyles to opinions. Conflicts can also create a divide in your team as those that are at ends will most likely try to include other employees.

Employee conflicts can be a drain on the team efficiencies and productivities, and as a manager or leader, it is your responsibility to address it. Disputes cannot go unmanaged as even simple arguments between employees can escalate into more significant issues. Also, if the situation is left unmanaged, it could have damaging impacts such as reduced productivity, the loss of key employees, and the loss of trust in your leadership.

When employee conflicts break out be prepared to work closely with both employees and or groups. The fact of the matter is that employees don't need to be friends, but they do have to work together to get the job done.

Although the word conflict seems to have a negative connotation, not all conflict has a negative result. Functional conflict is the type of conflict that arises when people brainstorm and share good ideas and positive outcomes come from the conflict. Some leaders actually encourage functional conflict by assigning "devil's advocate" roles to team members and inviting those characteristically known as naysayers to meetings.

Types of Conflicts

Intrapersonal Conflict

Intrapersonal conflict arises within a person. Intrapersonal conflict can arise because of differences in roles. A manager may want to oversee an employee's work, believing that such oversight is a necessary part of the job. The employee, on the other hand, may consider such extensive oversight to be micromanagement or evidence of a lack of trust. Role conflict, another type of intrapersonal conflict, includes having two different job descriptions that seem mutually exclusive. This type of conflict can arise if you're the head of one team but also a member of another team.

Interpersonal Conflict

Interpersonal conflict can occur between coworkers, managers and employees, or CEOs and their staff. Interpersonal conflict is a key source of stress. In particular, employees who have an agreeable personality and those who have less social support at work report fluctuations in their happiness levels in reaction to how much interpersonal conflict they experience on a daily basis.

Competition could be one major reason behind interpersonal conflict. Interpersonal conflict can also arise from personality or value differences. For example, one person's style may be to "go with the gut" on decisions, while another wants to make decisions based on facts. Many companies suffer because of interpersonal conflicts, and keeping conflicts centered around ideas rather than individual differences is important in avoiding a conflict escalation.

Intergroup Conflict

Intergroup conflict is conflict that takes place among different groups. Types of groups may include different departments or divisions in a company, an employee union, management, or competing companies that supply the same customers.

Intergroup conflict is often made even worse due to the individual tendency for in-group bias. This may occur in groups that are similar in sex, religion, age, or race, or in groups that are created by organizational structure. The resulting "us versus them" mentality is often the reason behind organizational and international conflict.

Listen to Both Sides

It is essential to get a full understanding of the situation and to listen to both sides of the argument. Initially you will want to listen to both sides separately. This will create an environment that they feel comfortable in speaking more freely.

Also it is important not to take sides initially. Sometimes it is easy to take sides depending on the situation to take a side, however, as a leader you need to be open to discussing this with both parties before jumping to conclusions.

Resolve it quickly

When an employee conflict occurs do not allow too much time to pass before addressing it with the employees. It is essential to address the concern as soon as possible.

Addressing the situation as quickly as possible also allows the employees to explain the situation better to you. As time passes, the more the story changes. Tensions can increase and fester among the employees, and the situation could get worse.

Encourage Employees to resolve it themselves

Depending on the type of argument and whether or not Human Resources needs to get involved, leave it up to the employees to resolve their conflicts.

Some arguments can be petty like a discussion over a politics or a favorite sports team. Make sure the employees understand that this is up to them to resolve the issue and that arguing at work is not acceptable.

Consult the Employee Handbook

Some arguments can cross the boundaries of what is acceptable in a workplace environment and what is not. If you feel that a line was crossed with one of the employees or both, it is essential to make sure policies are identified and enforced. If it is identified that policy was broken, you should reach out to your Human Resources department to get involved with the situation.

Teach, Practice, Repeat

As a leader, some situations can be learning ones for the employees. If a conflict occurs and you feel there is a process that can be followed to alleviate tensions work with the employees to coach them on the method or process.

Once you have shown them the process, it is crucial for them to perform it with you in a way that they can practice and have a full understanding. Work with the employee again and again until they feel comfortable performing the process or method.

Change the Composition of the Team

If the conflict is between team members, the easiest solution may be to change the composition of the team, separating the personalities that were at odds. In instances in which conflict is attributed to the widely different styles, values, and preferences of a small number of members, replacing some of these members may resolve the problem. If that's not possible because everyone's skills are needed on the team, and substitutes aren't available, consider a physical layout solution.

Research has shown that when known antagonists are seated directly across from each other, the amount of conflict increases. However, when they are seated side by side, the conflict tends to decrease

Create a Common Opposing Force

Group conflict within an organization can be mitigated by focusing attention on a common enemy, such as the competition. The "enemy" need not be another company—it could be a concept, such as a recession, that unites previously warring departments to save jobs during a downturn.

Consider Majority Rule

Sometimes a group conflict can be resolved through majority rule. That is, group members take a vote, and the idea with the most votes is the one that gets implemented. The majority rule approach can work if the participants feel that the procedure is fair. It is important to keep in mind that this strategy will become ineffective if used repeatedly with the same members typically winning.

Organizational Adjustments

If the situation cannot be resolved between the employees and both employees are good workers and good for the company, you may want to consider an organizational adjustment.

It is not uncommon to separate workers that cannot get along. Whether that means moving them to another department or having them work on another team, it may be the right thing to do for both them and the company.

Things to Avoid

Avoid Passing the Buck

Do not make an organizational adjustment if the employee is toxic, do not make that employee someone else's headache. Sometimes if the employee is toxic and has been identified as a repeat offender, then you may way to consider starting the process to move them out of the company.

Do not put the ownership of dealing with an employee conflict on another manager or Human Resources. It is best to handle the situation yourself as you are most likely most familiar with the people and the situation.

Don't Be the Only One Speaking

When speaking with your employees and listening to their side of the employee conflict, don't just wait for your turn to speak, allow them to explain their side of the situation thoroughly.

Never In Public

When confronting the employees do not do it in public make sure you are having all the conversations behind closed doors.

Remove Emotions

Keep emotions out of this. It is important to remain professional at all times and to keep a level head. Regardless of the situation, you must stay emotionally in control.

12
Dealing with Toxic Environments

"In every job and position, there are valuable lessons to be learned. Even in a nasty, abusive, toxic workplace, you're being taught precisely how not to run an organization."

- *Ryan Holiday*

A TOXIC ENVIRONMENT can make you feel uncomfortable, unappreciated or undervalued. This type of environment can come from your boss, your peers, other teams or even your employees. A toxic workplace can not only stifle one's career but it can also have adverse effects on their health.

While the dangers of a toxic environment are well known it can be difficult to identify and diagnose. All jobs have some level of stress, even on good days. As a leader in your organization is crucial that you identify the root cause of the toxic environment as quickly as possible.

Identify the Toxic Environment

There are a number of different red flags you should be looking for when you sense that the workplace environment you are working for is toxic. When it comes to your instincts in this situation, trust them.

If you feel like something is fishy at work, chances are you might be right. It is possible that the toxic environment is being created from the top down or on the other hand from the bottom up.

Lack of Transparency

Sometimes the job itself can be difficult and without receiving the proper feedback from your supervisor on how you are performing at your job may already be setting you up to fail. Lack of transparency in your job role or communications about your objectives make it almost impossible to have a mutually respectful, trusting relationship in the workplace.

Another area for lack of transparency can be demonstrated by a lack of communication where employees find out about a decision after it has been implemented. This usually stems from the top down and can cause mass confusion as well as a feeling of disconnect for your team.

Inconsistent Rulebook or Policies

It is important for any leader to ensure that the rulebook is being followed, however, when a leader hold one employee accountable but let's another employee get away with the same broken rule or behavior it comes across as favoritism.

When a company's policies and procedures are not followed, chaos, inconsistency and poor quality follow. Customers, vendors and employees wind up hating dealing with the company and its staff.

You're Being Bullied

With all of the education on this topic you would think this is a thing of the past, however, it runs rampant in toxic workplaces. Being mistreated by a supervisor or peer is just not acceptable. Any conduct that where you are repeatedly being threatened, humiliated, or intimidated need to be reported immediately.

A Punitive Environment

If you find you work in an environment where you have to keep your head down if you realize that if you make a mistake, criticize or make a suggestion you get attacked and or punished. This type of environment stifles creativity or innovation and increases worker stress.

Managers are Dictators

Having a dictator of a manager is a red flag that you are working in a toxic environment. This creates an environment of distrust and usually sends morale to an all-time low. This will suck the life out any team and usually has high turnover if this is not corrected.

Leadership Doesn't Support You

A good leader should be supporting your ideas, goals and aspirations. It is not uncommon for leaders to put their own interests first. Unfortunately it is not uncommon for some leaders prevent your growth and prevent you from promotions. This could be due to jealousy of your performance and start taking credit for your work. This of course undermines all of the hard work you are doing and if you identify this you need to get out of that situation as soon as possible.

How to Fix a Toxic Workplace

As a leader you need to ensure that your employees are in an environment in which supports them, encourages them, and is one in which they are productive and happy.

1. Identify Problem Behaviors

There are a number of warning signs that can be easily identified that could be turning your workplace toxic. Some common signs are:

- Gossiping or social cliques

- Bullying Behavior

- Excessive absenteeism, illness or fatigue

- High Turnover

- Imbalanced working conditions such as discriminatory policies or wage gaps

- Unrealistic workloads or deadlines

- Unsafe or morally questionable working conditions

- Everything that you or someone else does is criticized

- Employees are constantly fearing they will get fired

2. Evaluate

Once you have identified some of the behaviors in the workplace it is time to delve deeper and understand how these behaviors are being supported. You need to look at the company's leadership and their values. If you are new to the leadership role in this environment it may not always be clear. Be on the lookout for:

- Discriminatory beliefs

- Treating employees as assets, not people

- Information Guarding (Poor Communication or unclear expectations)

- Aggressive or hostile leadership styles

- Lack of Accountability

- Lack of Appreciation or recognition of good work

3. Plan Your Next Steps

Now that you have a clear understanding of the issues it is now time to start to plan your repair strategy. If there are multiple issues tackle the largest issues with the biggest impacts first. It is important that you:

- Listen to your employees – Set some time aside to ensure that you speak to all employees that are involved.

- Assign realistic workloads and deadlines – Work closer with your employees to understand how long it takes to perform tasks.

- Communicate Transparently – Set and manage expectations with your employees and teams.

- Acknowledge Good Work – Recognize an employee or a team when good work is accomplished or performed.

- Enforce the Rules for all Employees – Ensure that you are not playing favorites and that you have a clear understanding of the company polices so they can be enforced.

4. Implement your Plan

It is now time to execute your plan. At this point you have identified bad behavior and where it stems from. You have also engaged the employees that are involved. You understand that you need to create realistic workloads, communicate transparently, acknowledge and recognize good work and enforce all company policies equally.

In order to execute properly, you need to make sure that you have created new policies or standard operating procedures as needed. Ensure that you have setup regular team meetings and are communicating information to the team clearly. Implementing your strategic plan is as important, or even more important, than your strategy.

It is also important that you are holding all employees responsible and accountable for adhering to any changes you have made. If they fail to do so you need to understand why and handle accordingly.

5. Reflect and Change As Needed

Any changes, policies or processes that you have implemented should be given enough time to take root as changes will not happen overnight. It is important that you monitor the progress, and resist the urge to make any changes if only a little time has passed. After a couple of months have passed meet with the individuals you involved and reflect on how things have been going since the last change you have made.

Remember that any changes you have made can be further tweaked, modified or abolished completely as you see fit. Culture change is a big undertaking but if you invest the time to change a toxic environment to positive one your teams productivity will pay dividends.

Focus on Solutions Not Complaints

Nothing is more toxic and contagious than employees complaining. Whether it be bad-mouthing each other, company leadership or dress code policies, complaints show a mentality of defeat rather than feeling empowered by the company culture.

Do Not Avoid the Issues

The last thing you want to do is to avoid the issues especially after being able to identify an issue. Ignoring an issue will not make the situation go away and will most likely make the situation worse.

13
Written Corrections

"A coach is someone who can give correction without causing resentment."

-   *John Wooden*

WRITING SOMEONE UP is never an easy thing to do, but it is necessary to make sure the employee understands there is an issue. Making sure you are managing expectations for the employee is essential.

Just as recognition is important to reinforce positive behavior, if negative behavior has been identified it is equally important to punish the employee. It needs to be clear to the employee that there are consequences to negative behavior and as a leader you need to ensure employees understand there are rewards and punishments in the workplace.

When writing an employee up it is vital that you are not only making sure Human Resources is aware of the situation but that you are also following all the processes that they recommend. Written corrections usually take place after multiple verbal corrections have taken place.

Organizational Behavior Modification

You need to make sure you are making every attempt to modify the behavior of the employee to achieve the expected results. Organizational Behavior Modification or OB Mod is a reinforcement theory to modify an employee's behavior in the work force.

The OB Mod consists of five stages:

Step 1: It is important to identify the behavior that needs to be modified. For example, the employee has a problem with absenteeism.

Step 2: You need to be able to measure the baseline. In the example of the employee dealing with absenteeism, we need to identify how many times the employee has been absent, this week, this month, etc.

Step 3: It is important to analyze the antecedents and outcomes. You need to identify why the employee is absent and what are the impacts and effects on the team and the organization.

During this step you need to also make sure the employee is not being unintentionally rewarded. For example, if the employee is still getting paid or if they are avoiding unpleasant tasks or assignments which are being done by their employees.

Step 4: At this step you need to intervene, and writing up the employee up may be necessary.

Step 5: As a manager you need to make sure you are continually measuring the behavior periodically and is maintained.

Writing someone up

It Should Never Be A Surprise

If there is an ongoing issue, the employee should never be surprised. You want to make sure that you have had at the very least, one discussion regarding their performance before writing them up.

There should be constant communications, and updates regarding any employee deficiencies. This should not only be sent to the employee but also all stakeholders such as your supervisor and HR as needed.

Coaching and opportunities should be extended to the employee, so they have a chance to improve. It is important to remember that writing someone up does not necessarily mean that the employee is on their way out. The message to the employee must remain positive during this process, especially if they are improving.

Never Reprimand an Employee in Public

These conversations should never be in public and should be behind closed doors. Reprimanding an employee in public can create a negative environment.

Include HR When Needed

Make sure HR is involved and is aware of the process. It is important to make sure that they are involved just in case this situation escalates.

Follow your HR recommendations and processes. Most likely your organization already has processes and procedures to follow which will make your job during this process easier. Make sure you are following them!

Use Documentation

Ensure you are writing someone up based on a written policy/procedure/job description. This will help build a strong case and one that is easy for the employee to understand.

If needed create a process and procedure then train employees if one does not exist; Ensure division shareholders are involved.

Include Multiple People

If possible when having crucial conversations or writing up an employee try to include your supervisor as well.

Sometimes situations arise "he said / she said" and having a third party sit in can verify.

Performance Improvement Plan

Sometimes employees do not improve even after writing them up, ensure that it is recorded and implement a PIP (Process Improvement Plan). A PIP is a written plan to provide the employee with a roadmap to improve in areas they are having difficulties in.

Plans are usually 90 days and are then discussed with the employee at the end of 90 days. If the employee does not improve then termination is common.
Keep a lookout for a temporary improvement in productivity and attitude which is the psychological reaction. The change may be a temporary improvement, so it is essential to monitor this closely.

Things to Avoid

Stick With the Facts

Keep the personal impressions and conclusions out of the content and remain professional. When writing someone up avoid emotional content.

Spell Out the Consequences

Forgetting to include consequences for the undesired behavior is an issue. Clearly outlining the problem and the consequences, so the employee understands what will happen if this action is not corrected.

Remain Calm

Do not engage the employee in any heated exchange. Sometimes the employee may respond with anger or blame. Remain calm at all times.

Be Prepared

Not having the proper documentation readily available or having spotty documentation during the event can draw the process out. Make sure you have all necessary documentation that supports the employee being fired as well as all previous verbal warning documentation and prior write-ups.

14
Firing an Employee

"It's better to be alone than in bad company."

-   *George Washington*

FIRING SOMEONE is one of the hardest things that a leader has to do. I have never met a single person that gets some joy out of doing this task. It is one of the necessary functions that a leader must do for the greater good of the organization. If you do not feel that you have it in you to fire someone management may not be the best role for you as you will most likely have to do it at least once in your management role.

Firing someone usually takes time and is not something most employers can do on a whim. The process of firing someone could take weeks and even months. In most cases those employees that are poor performers need to have their performance tracked and recorded. Their performance needs to be measured and they must be provided opportunities to improve.

As you familiarize yourself with the process and procedure, it will get easier. The emotions you may have during the event will lessen over time, and the more you do this, the more comfortable you will become to those events. Again, it is essential to keep in mind that you are doing this for the better good of the organization and it should never be personal.

Terminating an Employee

Terminating an employee is one of the hardest things to do as a leader. I have never met a leader that enjoyed doing this but is part of the job that is necessary from time to time. If you feel you cannot make those types of decisions, then you shouldn't become a manager. It is a harsh reality that you will eventually have to make a difficult decision that can be life altering for the employee.

Do What is Right for the Company

It is important for you as a leader to do what is right for the company. While it is important to make sure the employee is happy and productive it equally important to ensure that the employees are performing their job as needed.

If the employee is not performing up to par and you have tried to improve their productivity without seeing any improvement it may be time to let the employee go. Keep in mind that if the company fails everyone is out of a job. There should really be no room in a company for those that cannot keep with the recommended minimum tasks.

Only Terminate an Employee When all else Fails

Coach, Coach, Coach! Make sure that they have been given every opportunity to succeed. Do not give up on the employee, remember, part of your role is to make sure your employees succeed.

If terminating an employee is unavoidable, push the employee out of the company rather than to another department. Transferring them to another department is not fair to the leadership of that area or to the organization.

Follow the process!

Make sure that you are following any rules and processes and keep in mind that HR is there to help, reach out to them as needed. Ensure all discrepancies are documented and submitted. You need to make sure that there is a record of all issues you have experienced with the employee. This will not only build a stronger case for you it will also ensure that you are protecting the organization.

Get HR Involved

While HR is in the room when someone is getting fired, <u>it is essential to make sure that there is at least one other person in the room,</u> such as another manager or your supervisor.

This prevents any he said / she said situations. It is not uncommon for employees to attempt to protect themselves at all costs as their job in most cases are their livelihood. Having someone in the room with you can back up how the situation went.

In rare cases it can get physical, it's always good to have another person in the room. If you feel that a physical altercation may occur with the employee and you have a security team it is good to have them on standby and are aware of the situation beforehand.

Do it behind closed doors.

Just like reprimanding someone, never fire anyone in public or in front of other employees. It is important for employees to feel comfortable in their work environment. If you feel comfortable firing someone in public, it sends a bad message to the rest of the employees.

Unless it is unavoidable, never fire someone over the phone, face to face is best. While it may be uncomfortable it is important to respect the employee even if they are on their way out.

Do not draw it out – Be Direct.

Explain why they are being terminated (which should never be a surprise). Be clear and concise with your message and avoid going off on a tangent.

Have them sign off on any paperwork as needed. It is not uncommon for employee to have to sign off on any confidentiality agreements or other organizational agreements. Make sure you understand the documents just in case they have any questions about them.

Collect any equipment from them, access badge, keys, etc. Make sure you do this immediately after firing someone as you may never see the items again.

Escort them off of the property or if needed have security assist. Do not allow them to roam and spend too much time speaking with people before they leave. You may find yourself in the middle of scene you do not want to be in.

Things to Avoid

Push Them Out

Pushing a poor performer to another department, don't give someone else your headache. It is always best to move poor performers out of your organization.

Keep a Record and Communicate

Don't fire an employee without warning. They should never feel blindsided when it comes down to terminating them, it is not uncommon to have repeat offenders regardless of the situation, make sure you are keeping a record and communicating and writing up the employee when an infraction occurs.

Collect All Company Property

In most cases, you should not allow the employee to leave until collecting all company property. You may never see that property back again.

Fire Them Yourself

Don't get someone else to do the dirty work. If it is your employee and they report to you, you should be the one to explain why they are being terminated.

This is NOT Personal

Again, you need to keep emotions and personal beliefs out of this. Don't allow this to become personal. This is just about business. Do not get defensive or engage in arguing with them.

15
Recognition

"People work for money, but go the extra mile for recognition, praise, and rewards."

- *Dale Carnegie*

THERE ARE A FEW THINGS that are more important to an employee's morale than recognition. Employees that are recognized are much happier as you demonstrate how much of an impact they have on your team and for the organization. As a leader, it is crucial that you create a culture of appreciation through recognition in your environment.

There is a strong connection between recognition and job satisfaction and leaders that recognize employees create strong bonds with their employees. This not only has positive impacts on the leader and the employee receiving the recognition, but it also affects peers who see good work being rewarded.

Creating an environment where an employee feels valued is one of the best ways to boost morale. If your company does not have a recognition program, work with either your Human Resource department or your fellow leaders as this will pay off with dividends.

Why is Recognition Important at Work?

Recognition communicates to employees that the work they do is valuable and appreciated. It drives greater levels of discretionary effort and your employees are inspired and willing to do more.

Recognition also drives employee retention and talent. It is important to have loyal employees as they are the future of your company.

Recognition reinforces the organization's values by identifying behavior that is in alignment with.

What can you recognize?

- Extra effort – presenting, taking on a project, helping a co-worker or another department.

- Any type of improvements that they recommend that is going to be implemented.

- Accomplishments that they have achieved which can either be personal or work-related.

- Tenure is a common one to celebrate, it also sends a good message to new employees that you appreciate loyalty.

- Birthdays are a good way to recognize your employees, do it with a lunch, a birthday cake or a celebration after work. Make sure to invite all employees!

- If available, give the employees a choice over rewards. Allowing them to provide feedback on what rewards are important to them is a great way to boost morale.

How to Recognize Performance

- Sometimes just saying thank you is enough to boost the employee's spirits.

- Know enough about employees as individuals so you may make the recognition most meaningful for them. i.e., Public versus Private, Oral versus Written

- Written notes (handwritten are more powerful). Send them to their home, so their family sees

- Make recognition a regular agenda item and perform it on quarterly, bi-annual or annual basis.

- Include family members when appropriate, having recognition for the employee not only shows them that you appreciate them, it also shows their family how important that employee is to the company or organization.

- Consider implementing a "Clutch" Award or something that recognizes a highly valued behavior.

- Use storytelling to share recognition with others in the organization.

- Consider that highly motivated employees are often rewarded by being given more challenging, high impact assignments and opportunities to experience professional development and visibility.

- Be sure to use the mechanisms already in place such as "Employee of the Quarter," "Wow" or "Bravo" type programs, Innovator's Award, Employee Referral. Make these more meaningful by adding additional words of recognition.

- Recognize team achievements through internal employee communications such as newsletters as well as the local community newspaper.

Things to Avoid

Reward Those Who Deserve It

Do not award someone for an issue or problem they have caused. It is always important to understand the root cause. It is important to remember that not everyone gets recognized unless they meet specific criteria.

Broadcast

Try not to recognize an achievement with just the employee. It is important to broadcast to the organization or during a meeting and treat it as a win for the team.

Know Your Employees

There is a flip side to recognizing and broadcasting the achievement. If you know the employee is an introvert and does not want to have, the achievement broadcasted to the entire organization. Send it out to a select few and recognize that individual in private.

Be Consistent

Make sure the recognition is consistent. If the employee recognition is inconsistent, for example, you recognize one employee one month for a win but then another employee does it a month later, and you do not recognize them, it can come across as favoritism.

Be Specific

Avoid only rewarding outcomes and goal achievement. Recognize specific behaviors and performance. Acknowledge effort as well as actual success.

16
Managing Generations

"Each generation goes further than the generation preceding it because it stands on the shoulders of that generation. You will have opportunities beyond anything we've ever know."

- *Ronald Reagan*

UNDERSTANDING the generational gaps between employees has been identified in recent years as an essential area of focus. While we will speaking in generalizations in this section, we do understand that each employee is unique and do not always fall into specific categories.

For the first time in history, five generations will be working side by side. It is essential to understand the generational gaps. Finding motivation differ for someone that is older to someone that is younger. It is also critical for a leader to be able to relate to different age groups. Lastly, you will want to encourage employees from different generations to share their knowledge.

Keep in mind that each generation brings with them a different set of skills, attitudes, and capabilities to a role. Managers overall need to be more flexible regarding their management style and change the way they communicate with their employees.

Over the next 30 years, 76 million baby boomers will retire, but there will only be 46 million new workers from Generations X and Y entering the labor force. This demographic trend creates both challenges and opportunities for organizations.

Defining Generations

Each generation can be defined by meeting certain criteria and label certain age groups.

The Silent Generation or Traditionalists

In most cases this generation was too young to see action in World War II and they were too old to participate in the fun of the Summer of Love. This generation believed that if you followed the rules and worked hard that you would be able to succeed and live the American Dream.

- Born 1928 – 1945

- Silents are considered among the most loyal workers.

- They are highly dedicated and the most risk-averse.

- Their values were shaped by the Great Depression, World War II, and the postwar boom years.

- Silents possess a strong commitment to teamwork and collaboration and have high regard for developing interpersonal communications skills.

The Baby Boom Generation

The boomers were born during an economic and baby boom following World War II. Vietnam War was a reality for this generation. They not only protested the Vietnam War but also participated in the civil rights movement. Rock and Roll was played a huge influence culturally for this generation.

- Born 1946 – 1964

- Boomers are the first generation to declare a higher priority for work over personal life actively.

- They generally distrust authority and large systems.

- Their values were shaped primarily by a rise in civil rights activism, Viet Nam, and inflation.

- They are more optimistic and open to change than the prior generation, but they are also responsible for the "Me Generation," with its pursuit of personal gratification, which often shows up as a sense of entitlement in today's workforce.

Generation X

They were originally called the baby busters because fertility rates fell after the boomers. As teenagers, they experienced the AIDS epidemic and the fall of the Berlin Wall. Sometimes called the MTV Generation, the "X" in their name refers to this generation's desire not to be defined.

- Born 1965 – 1980

- Generation Xers are often considered the "slacker" generation.

- They naturally question authority figures and are responsible for creating the work/life balance concept.

- Born in a time of declining population growth, this generation of workers possesses strong technical skills and is more independent than the prior generations.

- Gen Xers are willing to develop their skill sets and take on challenges and are perceived as very adaptive to job instability.

The Millennial Generation

They experienced the rise of the Internet, September 11th and the wars that followed. Sometimes called Generation Y because of their dependence on technology. They are viewed to be entitled and narcissistic by other generations.

- Born 1981- 1997

- This group is the first global-centric generation, having come of age during the rapid growth of the Internet and an increase in global terrorism.

- They are among the most resilient in navigating change while deepening their appreciation for diversity and inclusion.

- The Millennials are also the most educated generation of workers today.

- They represent the most team-centric generation since the Silents.

Generation Z

With Generation Z entering the workforce, they are the first generation in history to work along the side of four other generations. It is essential to start to get to know some traits of the next generation in the workforce.

This generation was the first born with the Internet and are suspected to be the most individualistic and technology-dependent generation. Sometimes referred to iGeneration or iGen and Post Millennials.

- Born 1998 – 2010

- They seem to be more private than the previous generation the Millennials. As an example apps like Snapchat and Whisper have seen explosive growth where Facebook has lost 25 percent of this demographic since 2011.

- They are multi-taskers and are taking it to the next level. They prefer to work on four computer screens not two like the millennials.

- They are technology-reliant; this one won't surprise you. Millennials are addicted to technology, get ready for more of the same as Generation Z. In surveys, they put technology in the same category as air and water.

Generation Alpha

- Born 2010 – TBD

- They will be more self-sufficient, better educated and prepared for big challenges. Gen Alpha will have to take on many of the biggest challenges of the world.

- They will be the most tech savvy and not know a world without social networking. Alpha's will be introduced to mobile phones before becoming teenagers and will take most of the technology we use today for granted.

- Their mobile phones will be so sophisticated when they become teenagers that they will primarily use their phone over a laptop or desktop computer.

Understanding and Managing by Generation

Communication

- Silents and Baby Boomers may appreciate verbal communication about changes in policy or procedures.

- Generation Xers and Millennials may prefer the use of e-mail, instant messages, or corporate broadcasts.

Attractions

- As more Silents retire, Baby Boomers seek "Postretirement careers."

- Gen Xers demand challenging but balanced work assignments

- Millennials and Generation Z's expect big perks in exchange for loyalty and are technologically savvy. Leaders must find creative ways to recruit and retain talent.

Mentoring Generations

Consider various mentoring models—one-on-one sessions, group programs, senior leadership discussion panels, and a "speed mentoring" program where employees sit across from company experts to ask questions.

No matter what method you choose, making mentoring a part of the employment lifecycle will ensure that the company's history and knowledge continues from one generation to the next. Keep in mind the manager styles, as they are the same regardless of the generation you come from, and that very few managers or leaders are just one style overall.

Silents

For Silents, mentoring was an obligation—they were the senior leaders who were asked to step up as mentors.

Baby Boomers

Baby Boomers were the generation seeking out mentorship, which led them to view mentoring as a way to get ahead.

Gen Xers

Generation X started pushing Baby Boomers to experiment with virtual relationships and electronic communication. Gen X wanted to engage in more virtual mentoring, and they also want to collaborate more efficiently with their peers.

Millennials

For Millennials, mentoring is merely collaborative, and networked learning that includes many people. It is a process where they use technology to connect with people across an organization so that they can share critical knowledge and skills, and solicit advice and opinions from people with diverse backgrounds.

Millennials determine their goals and developmental needs, and then pair them with older, more experienced employees to create cross-organizational dialogue among generations.

Generation Z

Remember that Generation Z's are digital natives. With this generation, they do not know a world without the internet. In many cases, they grew up with an iPad or another tablet in hand. In most cases, they are connected with their peers all day every day.

Gen Zers expect the workplace to conform to their needs. They are similar to millennials in this way, and are actually fairly similar to boomers as well. This attitude is having an effect on the workplace.

Generation Alpha

The business world is going to be confronted with the most demanding customers and employees in history, expecting speed, responsiveness and customization as a standard: an app-style service from any business they choose to have a relationship with.

As employees, Alphas will be tougher to keep motivated and challenged. In response, many types of work will become more like a series of individual projects and challenges with their own rewards.

Things to Avoid

Avoid Blanket Stereotypes

Understand that even though there are certain traits for each generation, it is important to remember that your employees are individuals and do not necessarily always fall into categories or have specific characteristics.

The More Things Change, The More They Stay The Same

Keep in mind that new generations will encounter some of the same issues their older counterparts have faced when entering the workforce. It is important not to overanalyze be overly romantic or too critical about new generations.

Made In The USA

The generations that were covered in this section are generations here in the United States. Keep in mind any employees that are not native to America do not necessarily reflect the traits covered.

SECTION 4

UNDERSTAND YOUR ROLE

Role (Noun) rōl - A function or part performed especially in a particular operation or process

Synonyms: business, capacity, function, job, part, place, position, purpose, task, work;

17
Implementing Change

"Change can be frightening, and the temptation is often to resist it. But change almost always provides opportunities – to learn new things, to rethink tired processes, and to improve the way we work."

- *Klaus Schwab*

CHANGE MANAGEMENT is another problematic area for managers to overcome. This can be as tense a situation as writing someone up or firing someone. Change is enviable in any environment, whether it is strategic, leadership or technological changes. It is essential to be cautious when discussing the change with employees.

Communicating change needs to be done formally with your employees which in turn tells them why the change is happening, what they should expect, and how the change will benefit them. It is essential to keep employees involved from the start to help with a smooth transition.

Ultimately people fear the unknown and can be initially resistant to it. However, over time by keeping the communication open it will help build trust with your team. Change management can be challenging, and it is essential to understand how to handle the change and understand what the employee may be thinking and or feeling.

Creating Culture Change

There are a few steps that can be followed to successfully change culture in your organization. Changing a company's culture may be the key to the company's turnaround if there is a mismatch between an organization's values and the demands of its environment.

Communicate Effectively

It is essential to keep the message consistent whenever a change is discussed, so the same message is presented. Having too many separate meetings with employees may convey different understandings of the change.

Be transparent if possible, call a meeting to break the message with the team and then have a follow-up meeting to discuss the details. In order for a change effort to be successful, it is important to communicate the need for change to employees. One way of doing this is to create a sense of urgency on the part of employees and explain to them why changing the fundamental way in which business is done is so important.

Change Key Players

A leader's vision is an important factor that influences how things are done in an organization. Thus, culture change often follows changes at the highest levels of the organization. Moreover, in order to implement the change effort quickly and efficiently, a company may find it helpful to remove managers and other powerful employees who are acting as a barrier to change.

Role Model

Role modeling is the process by which employees modify their own beliefs and behaviors to reflect those of the leader. The ultimate goal is that these behaviors will trickle down to lower level employees. When positive role modeling is executed at top levels, it is likely to have an positive impact on the company culture.

Train

Well-crafted training programs may be instrumental in bringing about culture change by teaching employees new norms and behavioral styles. Customer reports have been overwhelmingly positive in stores that underwent this training

Change the Reward System

The criteria with which employees are rewarded and punished have a powerful role in determining cultural values. Rewarding employees who embrace the company's new values and even promoting these employees, organizations can make sure that changes in culture have a lasting impact.

Create New Symbols and Rituals

The success of the culture change effort may be increased by developing new rituals, symbols, and stories. By replacing the old ones, new symbols and stories will help enable a culture change and ensure that the new values are communicated.

The Seven Stages of Grief

Change can be so difficult for most people that they go through the seven stages of grief. It is important to remember this when evoking significant changes with an individual or group of employees.

Depending on the employee they may go through this very quickly, or it may take some time depending on the individual.

7 Stages of Grief Model

1. **SHOCK & DENIAL** - The employee will probably react to learning of this change with numbed disbelief. They may deny the reality of the change at some level. Shock provides emotional protection from being overwhelmed all at once.

2. **PAIN & FRUSTRATION** - As the shock wears off, it is replaced with the suffering pain. It may make them feel sick to their stomach or give them headaches. They may start to become frustrated with the loss of control over the situation.

3. **ANGER & BARGAINING** - Frustration gives way to anger, and they may lash out and lay unwarranted blame. This is a time for the release of bottled up

emotion.

4. **"DEPRESSION," REFLECTION, LONELINESS -** This is a normal stage of grief, and encouragement from others may not be helpful during this stage.

5. **THE UPWARD TURN -** Physical symptoms lessen, and your "depression" begins to lift slightly.

6. **RECONSTRUCTION & WORKING THROUGH -** As they become more functional, their mind starts working again, and they can start seeing the bigger picture. Logic begins to regain a footing.

7. **ACCEPTANCE & HOPE -** During this, the last of the seven stages, you learn to accept and deal with the reality of your situation. Acceptance does not necessarily mean instant happiness. You will find a way forward.

How to Respond To Some Employee Emotions

Denial

Behaviors to expect to see	Actions to Help the Employee
Flip attitude	1. Share accurate information again and again;
Indifferent Talk	2. Ask questions;
Evasion	3. Explain the change and the reasons;
Skepticism	4. Give examples of peers who are changing, learning;
Refusal to Accept the Situation	5. Provide examples of the need for this new system / approach / technology;

Anger

Behaviors to expect to see	Actions to Help the Employee
Grumbling	1. Listen;
Irritation	2. Acknowledge anger;
Mistakes	3. Do not talk them out of it;
Passive-Aggressive	4. Do not assume blame for their anger;
Foot-Dragging	5. In rare cases, if real harm is possible, consult security / ER experts.

Bargaining

Behaviors to expect to see	Actions to Help the Employee
Trying to get out of the situation Make it Go Away Making a Deal or Promise Negotiation	1. Keep the realistic plan in sight; 2. Don't be influenced by promises or negotiations; 3. Reinforce the situation as it is; 4. Gently remind them of reality;

Sadness

Behaviors to expect to see	Actions to Help the Employee
Silence Disheartened Tearful	1. Acknowledge; 2. Sympathize; 3. Encourage talking and sharing feelings either 1:1 or in a supportive group; 4. Probe with questions to understand; 5. Refer to professional;

Anxiety

Behaviors to expect to see	Actions to Help the Employee
Stressed Spreading Rumors Nervous Productivity lowered	1. Understand and acknowledge the feelings of loss, even if they seem like overreactions. 2. Encourage talking and listen carefully; 3. Do not talk them out of feelings, but offer a different point of view if you have one. 4. Give positive feedback on their progress, if genuine.

Depression

Behaviors to expect to see	Actions to Help the Employee
Downcast Signs of Fatigue Despair Ineffectiveness	1. Empathize and reach out; 2. Initiate conversation and ask questions to draw them out. 3. Promote supportive group events or interaction, impromptu fun.

1. **Structure the team to maximize its potential** - Give team members appropriate roles and responsibilities that use skills to their best advantage, while also providing the potential for personal and team development.

2. **Set challenging, achievable, and engaging targets** - Be clear in guidance about goals and objectives. Break change projects into smaller milestones, and celebrate achievements. Goals should be seen as progressive and in line with values and beliefs.

3. **Resolve conflicts quickly and effectively** - Utilize the seven methods of care-fronting to regulate and control communicative breakdowns. Encourage openness and honesty and engender an environment of mutual trust and respect.

4. **Show passion** - Communicate passionately and be an example of belief in the future vision.

5. **Be persuasive** - Engage employees in change by being an energized leader. Focus on opportunities and persuade rather than assert authority. Share experiences as you influence change through stories that focus on positive change.

6. **Empower innovation and creativity** - Give opportunities for feedback and remain flexible as you alter course toward your change goals. Encourage

people to be creative, discover solutions to unfolding problems, and to become part of the change process. The process is complicated for everyone involved, and your team will be more invested with solutions they have created themselves, rather than those dictated to them.

7. **Remain positive and supportive** - People find change unsettling, even though change is a constant in personal lives as well as professional environments. They will need the support of a confident leader who inspires free thought, honest communication, and creativity as individual and team development is encouraged.

Things to Avoid

Things You Should Never Say

Top 5 Things you should never say when discussing the change with an employee.

1. "I have no idea why *they* are making this change."

2. "Well...there is nothing we can do about it- we just need to go along with it."

3. "This is yet another example that they have no idea what we do out here on the floor."

4. "I agree with you, and I don't like it either."

5. "In all my years…this has got to be the stupidest decision *they* have ever made."

Be Clear

Not articulating the need for a change can confuse your employees. Make sure your team understands the reason behind the change.

Have A Plan

Not having an action plan or providing your employees a roadmap is another way to confuse employees. Without clear direction, your change management initiative could go nowhere.

Shotgun Management

A style of management characterized by frequent and massive changes, without really understanding what the results may be.

There is nothing wrong with trying something new or trying to change a process, however doing this too frequently could cause confusion and chaos is your department.

Pay Attention

During a change, employees may be feeling stressed and anxious about their job security. If the manager, not recognizing this, gives a lot of technical details about the timing and logistics of the change or how the change will benefit the organization, it may result in mistrust in management as the employees' feelings of anxiety are not being recognized and addressed.

18
Project Management

"Those who govern, having much business on their hands, do not generally like to take the trouble of considering and carrying into execution new projects. The best public measures are therefore seldom adopted from previous wisdom, but forced by the occasion."

- *Benjamin Franklin*

AS A MANAGER AND LEADER in any organization, the job is not just about managing people and day to day operations it is also about managing projects. Regardless of the size of the project, it is essential to stay organized and keep the project on track.

Projects in and out of themselves can be very stressful for not only you as a leader but also for your team. There are numbers of different ways to tackle and approach a project. Over time you will find what works best for you that will help you manage, keep track and organize your projects.

Great project management is about delivering on time, budget and scope. It is about uniting your ream and being able to create a clear vision for success and gets everyone on the same page. When projects are managed properly there is a positive impact that reverberates throughout your team and your organization.

Get Organized and Stay Organized

Develop an effective filing system

While paperwork is unavoidable in most projects as some information does require signatures, it is essential to keep it organized.

Create a folder or binder for all critical paperwork, if you must keep them as a hard copy. If possible scan all paperwork and create a filing structure on a computer and keep all correspondence in the folder as well.

Create specific spreadsheets and documents as needed

There is no need to reinvent the wheel. Use templates that you may have used on other projects.

Scour the web for templates that others have created to assist with project management.

Checklists are also a great way to identify who owns a specific task and whether or not it has been completed.

Use Project Management Software

If you have a budget for software, use it! There is plenty of excellent project management software out there.

Do yourself a favor, stick with a name brand. Unless someone highly recommends software stick with a reputable company and some software can be a waste of time and money.

Ultimately, Use What Work for You

Use tools that work for you, whether that is a computer, tablet, phone, pen or paper, post-it notes, etc. You know yourself better than anyone else, use what you feel comfortable with. You don't need to have the most expensive equipment out there, if you don't feel comfortable using it a pen an notepad work just as well.

Define the Goals and Objectives

It is essential to make sure that you are defining the scope of work early on in the project and are also setting expectations with your teams and stakeholders.

- Make sure you understand what the expected outcome or output of the project.

- Determine any costs and budgets associated with the project.

- Understanding the timeframe and deadlines that you need to meet to complete the project

- Determine the available resources you have about such as employee resources and financial resources

- Break down the tasks into smaller subgroups before tasking to anyone any objectives. This will help the team member met milestones.

Identify Team Strengths and Weaknesses

Make sure you get to know your team. By identifying strengths and weaknesses, you can make sure the right task is delegated to the right person.

Set expectations, set expectations, set expectations. It is crucial that your team knows what you expect of them. If someone on your team is consistently not meeting expectations, then they may not be the best person for the task, and it may need to be reassigned.

Communicate

Communication is a crucial component when leading a project. You will want to make sure that you are frequently meeting with both your teams and stakeholders on a regular interval.

Setup weekly/bi-weekly or monthly meetings and increase or decrease your intervals as needed. Make sure there is an agenda and that you make the meetings matter.

Send out emails as needed and be specific. Make sure your email as crucial information such as important dates/times, product information, names, etc.

Adjust Accordingly

You should anticipate issues as some always pop up. If you understand that there are will always some obstacles that arise when they do happen you will be less stressed about it.

When problems arise, it is essential to get all key stakeholders and team members to the table to discuss a solution to the problem.

Delegate someone to fix the issue, whether that is yourself or someone else, make sure an owner is assigned.

Things to Avoid

Manage Expectations

When communicating out to your team or to an individual regarding a project or a certain expectation it is crucial to communicate the expectations. If you lack details, it could cause the employee undue stress or misunderstand the request.

Use Reminders, Don't Rely on Memory Alone

Do not attempt to use your memory. Time slips away from us all. Emergencies come up, and people divide your attention. Make sure you are using reminders and set alarms on your calendar.

Build a Solid Team

Build a team based on experience and with those that have specific skill sets and not just on who is available. If you are only using "warm bodies" then it is likely that your team will not be highly proficient at the tasks at hand.

Communicate Properly

Poor communication with your team can cause major setbacks to the projects and could throw off the timeline. There is no excuse for failing to communicate with everyone.

Delegate

Don't do everything yourself! Make sure you are delegating out tasks as needed. You are supposed to be managing the project which is already taking up a lot of your time.

Don't Own Everything

Do not micromanage the team. This can cause conflict with the owners of the tasks that have been given out. When you give the appropriate tasks to the right people, let them own the work.

19
Negotiating

"Let us never negotiate out of fear. But let us never fear to negotiate."

- *John F. Kennedy*

THERE ARE TIMES IN ALL BUSINESSES as well as daily life where you must negotiate. Negotiating isn't always so easy, but it is an essential skill that you need to work on as a modern business professional. It is not uncommon for people to get caught in the moment and let their emotions take over.

Negotiating requires give and take. You should aim to create a courteous and constructive interaction that is a win-win for both parties. Ideally a successful negotiation is where you can make concessions that mean little to you, while giving something to the other party that means a lot to them.

The Five Phases of Negotiation

A common way that parties deal with conflict is via negotiation. There are five phases of negotiation, which are described below.

Phase One: Investigation

The first step in negotiation is investigation, or information gathering. This is a key stage that is often ignored. Surprisingly, the first place to begin is with yourself: What are your goals for the negotiation? What do you want to achieve? What would you concede? What would you absolutely not concede?

During the negotiation, you'll inevitably be faced with making choices, and it's best to know what you want so that in the heat of the moment you're able to make the best decision.

Phase Two: Determine Your BANTA

One important part of the investigation and planning phase is to determine your BATNA, which is an acronym that stands for the "best alternative to a negotiated agreement." Roger Fisher and William Ury coined this phrase in their book, *Getting to Yes: Negotiating Agreement Without Giving In.*

Thinking through your BATNA will help you decide whether to accept an offer you receive during the negotiation. You need to know what your alternatives are, and if you have various alternatives, you can look at the proposed deal more critically.

Phase Three: Presentation

The third phase of negotiation is presentation. In this phase, you assemble the information you've gathered in a way that supports your position. In a job hiring or salary negotiation situation, for instance, you can present facts that show what you've contributed to the organization in the past (or in a previous position), which in turn demonstrates your value.

Phase Four: Bargaining

During the bargaining phase, each party discusses its goals and seeks to make an agreement. A natural part of this process is making concessions. Making a concession is not a sign of weakness—parties expect to give up some of their goals. Rather, concessions demonstrate cooperativeness and help move the negotiation toward its conclusion.

Phase Five: Closure

Closure is an important part of negotiations. At the close of a negotiation, you and the other party have either come to an agreement on the terms, or one party has decided that the final offer is unacceptable and therefore must be walked away from. Most negotiators assume that if their best offer has been rejected, there's nothing left to do. You made your best offer, and that's the best you can do. The savviest of negotiators, however, see the rejection as an opportunity to learn: "What would it have taken for us to reach an agreement?"

Sometimes, at the end of negotiations, it's clear why a deal was not reached. But if you're confused about why a deal did not happen, consider making a follow-up call. Even though you may not win the deal back in the end, you might learn something that's useful for future negotiations.

Focus On Agreements First

If you reach an impasse during negotiations, sometimes the best recourse is to agree that you disagree on those topics and then focus only on the ones on which you can reach an agreement. Summarize what you've agreed upon, so that everyone is on the same page, and leave out the points where you don't agree. Then take up those issues again in a different context, such as over dinner or coffee.

Be Patient

If you don't have a deadline by which an agreement needs to be reached, use that flexibility to your advantage. The other party may be forced by circumstances to agree to your terms, so if you can be patient you may be able to get the best deal.

Deadlines

Research shows that negotiators are more likely to strike a deal by making more concessions and thinking more creatively as deadlines loom than at any other time in the negotiation process.

Silence is Golden

After you have made an offer, allow the other party to respond. Many people become uncomfortable with silence and feel like they need to say something. Wait and listen instead.

Understand Cultural Differences

Not understanding cultural differences is another common mistake made in negotiations. Some cultures have a higher or lower threshold for conflict. What works as a best practice in one culture may not work in a different culture. Even the way that negotiations are viewed can differ across cultures. For example, Western cultures tend to think of negotiations as a business activity rather than a social activity, but in other cultures, the first step in negotiations is to develop a trusting relationship.

Mediation

In mediation, an outside third party (the mediator) enters the situation with the goal of assisting the parties in reaching an agreement. The mediator can facilitate, suggest, and recommend, working with both parties to reach a solution but not representing either side. Rather, the mediator's role is to help the parties share feelings, air and verify facts, exchange perceptions, and work toward agreements.

Arbitration

In contrast to mediation, in which parties work with the mediator to arrive at a solution, in arbitration the parties submit the dispute to the third-party arbitrator. It is the arbitrator who makes the final decision. The arbitrator is a neutral third party, but the decision made by the arbitrator is final (the decision is called the "award").

Arbitration-Mediation

It is common to see mediation followed by arbitration, but an alternative technique is to follow the arbitration with mediation. The format of this conflict resolution approach is to have both sides formally make their cases before an arbitrator. The arbitrator then makes a decision and places it in a sealed envelope. Following this, the two parties work through the mediation. If they are unable to reach an agreement on their own, the arbitration decision becomes binding.

Things to Avoid

Avoid Playing Hardball

A good rule of thumb is that hardball tactics should not be used because the negotiation is not likely to be the last time you will interact with the other party. Therefore, finding a way to make a deal that works for both sides is preferable. Otherwise, if you have the complete upper hand and use it to "destroy" the other party, it's likely that at a future date the other party will have the upper hand and will use it to retaliate mercilessly against you.

Remove Your Ego

Thinking only about yourself is a common mistake. People from the United States tend to fall into a self-serving bias in which they overinflate their own worth and discount the worth of others. This can be a disadvantage during negotiations. Instead, think about why the other person would want to accept the deal. People aren't likely to accept a deal that doesn't offer any benefit to them.

Having Unrealistic Expectations

Setting unrealistic expectations is a quick way to kill any negotiation. Setting expectations that are too far out of reach or for asking for way too much can easily insult the people you are attempting to come to terms with.

Failing to Negotiate / Accepting the First Offer

Researchers calculate that people who routinely negotiate salary increases will earn over $1 million more by retirement than people who accept an initial offer every time without asking for more. The good news is that it appears that it is possible to increase negotiation efforts and confidence by training people to use effective negotiation skills.

Becoming Too Emotional

Negotiations, by their very nature, are emotional. The findings regarding the outcomes of expressing anger during negotiations are mixed. Those who express anger negotiate worse deals than those who do not.

Not Letting Go of the Past

Those who were unable to negotiate some type of deal in previous negotiation situations tended to have lower outcomes than those who had successfully negotiated deals in the past. The key to remember is that there is a tendency to let the past repeat itself. Being aware of this tendency allows you to overcome it.

Avoiding Conflict

Nothing ever good comes from avoiding conflict. Not dealing with an issue could very easily cause an issue to worsen overtime. It is not uncommon for conflict to start small but become a disaster later on.

20
Networking

"If you want to go fast, go alone. If you want to far, go together."

- African Proverb

THERE ARE MANY REASONS why networking is so vital for your career. Being a connected manager or leader and improving your network skills can help you climb up that career ladder.
Networking is not about just adding people to your social circles, or a popularity contest, it is about connecting with the right people.

Networking is also a great way to learn from not only the success of others but also what not to do. It is a great way to increase and expand your knowledge. There is an old saying that "iron sharpens iron" and networking around the right company is a great way to sharpen your skills.

There is another old saying, "it's not what you know, it's who you know." I disagree with the first half of that statement because making sure you are knowledgeable in your business is critical for a strong leader, but, increasing your network by growing your connections can really open doors of opportunities that generally would either not exist or are difficult to open.

You want to make sure you are networking correctly. It is essential that you create a healthy business relationship with that person. It is very much about respect and being able to reciprocate resources and assets and that you are sharing them accordingly.

You need to be aware of a couple of areas that you should pay attention or focus on to build your network successfully.

Your Reputation

While networking is really not about making friends, you need to give some thought to what other people think of you. While you may have been brought up and taught that it doesn't really matter what people think of you, but it does when networking.

Once you decide on what type of leader you want others to see you as it will help you work towards that goal. For example, you may want to be recognized as a leader that is innovative or collaborative, or perhaps results-driven. Identify what you want to be known for and take actions to get you where you want to be.

Be Self-Aware

Remember that you have a brand and a reputation, you need to have a strong sense of self-awareness. Identify your strengths and use them. Identify your weaknesses and improve upon them.

Superior Performance

Be consistent with exceeding expectations, not just meeting expectations. If you are recognized as someone who is consistently exceeding expectations, then you will be known as someone that has high potential.

Understand You

It is essential to have a clear understanding on what you do, why you do it, who you do it for and what you special for doing it. You would be surprised how many people struggle with explaining this. It is essential to not only know it but be able to articulate it.

Follow Through

It is essential for others to view you as helpful and thoughtful. Helping others is a great way to have others identify you as dependable and resourceful, however, if you do not follow through on what you would say you would do you can quickly fall from grace and end up on their wrong side. If you are going to offer help, you must follow through and follow up with the individual that requested your assistance.

Your Alliances

It is crucial for a leader to make sure you have strong alliances. While some associations may be brief other may last throughout your career. Regardless of how long certain alliances last having a good partner and a strong partnership is a key corporate asset to have.

Business Objective

From a sales standpoint, it is essential to have a strong strategic alliance as it can help grow your customer base. If you are looking to expand it a new market having a strong alliance can strengthen your position and improve your business space to continue to grow.

Additional Resources

With all of the resources that you use on a daily basis to be successful in your business have a strong alliance that can help support your needs with additional resources is a great way to use to your advantage when needed. Keep in mind that you need to balance this and not take advantage of any assistance and it is give and take.

Building a variety of alliances can help you in many different areas. To name a few examples of strategic relationships could be in marketing, technology, sales, supply chain, and vendor, etc.

Don't Compromise Your Values

It is essential that there is chemistry between you and your strategic alliances. Ensuring that you are working and aligning with like-minded individuals makes sure that your fundamental values are not compromised. When you compromise against your better judgement, your values can suffer.

We are living in the age of social media. According to Pew Research Center's survey, 73% of all internet users use social networking sites. Whether we like it or not, many people live their lives online now. We have fewer expectations of privacy, we are more likely to write about what we see than talk about it, and everything we do and say online has a broader audience.

Companies are paying attention to not only applicant's social media presences, but also to their employee's social media presence. Companies are consistently screening candidates based on their online presence. Online behavior that you demonstrate could not only prevent you from getting a job it can also cause you to lose your job.

Regardless of whether or not you agree that organizations should monitor employee behavior online there are no laws that bar it. Social media is a great way to connect with employees, employers and organizations and is a great way to network. It is important to remember that people have strong opinions and your presence online could prevent you from making excellent contacts.

Keep your Brand Clean

Understand that you have a professional brand, one that potential employers may see when they try to research who you are social media. It is essential to keep it professional at all costs as some posts could paint a lousy picture.

Have you Googled yourself lately? If not, you probably should. Potential employers have begun searching the web as part of background checks, and you should be aware of what's out there about you. It's possible to set up automated reports with Google so that every time your name (or any other term) is mentioned on the web, you are alerted.

Things to Avoid

Avoid Negativity

While avoiding adverse situations are not always possible, it is a good habit to avoid keeping company with negative people. Surrounding yourself with positive and uplifting people will help you grow and thrive. Remember "misery likes company."

Me, Myself and I

It can be easy to think only about your needs, but remember that networking is all about reciprocating. If you end up taking more than you give you can find yourself alone. You'll see the more you reciprocate, the more likely someone will help you when you need a favor.

Don't Fake It

It is essential to the best version of yourself. However, it is also equally important to make sure you have honest interactions. You do not want to build yourself up artificially. Be the best version of yourself and be true to who you are.

Religion and Politics

Sure you have heard it before, and maybe you have been burned by this but never, ever, in a business environment bring up religion and politics unless you are sure you are speaking to like-minded individuals. You will wind up offending and alienating someone that could have been a staunch ally.

Avoid the Gossip

It's always good to be recognized as someone that has a pulse on the department or organization, or someone that is "in the know." However, you can easily be marked as the department gossip king or queen. Keep the gossip and banter to a minimum otherwise you may find yourself in an awkward position, and you run the risk of losing a strong network contact.

21
Next Steps

"The only way to get started is to quit talking and begin doing."

- ***Walt Disney***

YOU SHOULD ALAWYS BE THINKING of your next steps and are continually be looking forward. Advancing your career falls solely on yourself. Unless you feel that the company that you work for is not the right fit for you it is best to set your focuses on an environment you are familiar with and start seeing what opportunities are available.

Areas of Focus

Identify Your Next Role

You should take a look at the landscape around you, and determine which role you would like for your next step. It provides you with a goal to achieve. You can start to devise a plan for what you need to do to meet that goal.

Find a Mentor

Identifying a mentor and start working closely with one. This is a great way to get feedback and identify some areas that you may need to focus in on. They will help you hone your skills which in return will make you more competent at your job.

Find a Boss

This one is easier said than done, however if you can find the right boss it can work wonders for your career. Ideal bosses don't care about control as they help other achieve their objectives. They create an environment in which education and knowledge building is encouraged. Ideal bosses also welcomes ideas from their employees which can bring out the best in people. Not only do great bosses inspire their employees they also believe in them.

One of the easiest ways to find a boss is if you are already working for a company and you can see the environment around you. If however you are on the outside looking in, visit sites like glassdoor.com and linkedin.com to get perspective and feedback.

Education

Ensure that your education is current, you find that you need to update a certificate, get a different one or finally get that diploma, and there is no better time than now to get started. Depending on the company, most offer educational reimbursement, use it to your advantage.

Identifying Your Replacement

From day one in your role, you should be identifying your replacement as it will take some time to get them up to speed. Once you have identified your replacement, you then need to start making them your right-hand person. By keeping them close, providing those tasks that may be slightly outside of the job role will better prepare them for their next position and will give you a better idea on where their strengths and weaknesses are.

Keep your Resume Updated

Make sure you are always updating and developing your resume. Remember that you are marketing yourself and if you do not provide a favorable impression it could sink some of your chances. Avoid using templates, and if you are struggling with creating a resume, it is worth it to have a professional help work with you on one.

Practice Interviewing

It is a good habit when preparing for an interview to see if your mentor or peer can help you run through a few practice interviews. Interviews can be nerve-racking any getting some practice time before the event can calm the nerves and provide you a better chance at having a successful interview.

Demonstrate a Strong Work Ethic

It is also good to demonstrate a strong work ethic. Showing your team that you have a strong work ethic indicates that you are committed to the goals and objectives. It also shows that you are striving to be successful in your work environment.

Don't Hold Yourself Back

You may feel pushed by your employer to take on the next role, or you may want to stay in your current position to get more exposure. There are times when you should take the leap to the next level as you may not know when the next opportunity will arise. Depending on your personality you may never fully feel ready for your future role but don't let that hold you back.

Sometimes we can be our own worst enemies. You need to be continually assessing yourself and try to figure what you may want from your next role.

Watch Out For Bad Bosses

It is essential that you have the support of your boss. Having the support of your boss can either make or break your career. If you are working for a boss that doesn't feel like they are mentoring you and getting you ready for your next step talk with them and make sure they understand your needs. If they are still not supportive, see if there is another team you can join with a positive reputation.

Dead End Positions

There are a few signs that you may be in a dead end job. It is essential to keep a lookout, and if you identify that you are in one, it is up to you to get yourself out of that situation.

1. Your manager can't identify a path for your growth within the company or if your manager has little or no interest in your career development.

2. The company's growth has slowed down. When a company's revenue slows down, there are generally fewer opportunities. It is crucial you are attending those financial meetings and paying attention to the reports.

Conclusion

"Leadership is about vision and responsibility, not power."

- **Seth Berkley**

MANY ELEMENTS HAVE BEEN COVERED in this book, which discussed certain areas that you should put focus on as a leader. While we have covered many techniques and provided you some insight try to focus on and practice only a few items each week. Over the course of a few months, you will find yourself becoming stronger in your role.

The techniques, models, and best practices that were covered are just are meant for you to take the basic concept and make it your own. We each have our styles, talents, strengths, and weakness that make us unique. So I hope this information points you in the right direction to make you the best leader you can be.

Keep in mind that only you have control over your path and if you are driven enough and with the right team, you can and will move mountains.

Index

Rounding 63

S

Sadness 141
Self-Control 12
Servant Leadership 16, 18
Seven Stages of Grief 138
Silent Generation 125
Social Media 165
Social Roles 74

T

Team Identity 78, 79
Team Management 69
Team Roles 73
Team Strengths 150
Team Weaknesses 150
Teleconference 48
Terminating 114 - 117
Time Blocking 42
Time Management 40 - 46
Toxic Environment 24, 99
Traditionalist Generation 125
Transactional Leadership 16
Trust 19, 25, 75, 76

V

Visionary 14

W

Web conference 48
Written Correction 107

Made in the USA
Middletown, DE
02 March 2019